GIRLS IN TROUBLE

Jonathan Reynolds

BROADWAY PLAY PUBLISHING INC
New York
www.broadwayplaypublishing.com
info@broadwayplaypublishing.com

Cover art by David Prittie
First printing: September 2010
I S B N: 978-0-88145-461-1
Book design: Marie Donovan
Typographic controls & page make-up: Adobe InDesign
Typeface: Palatino
Printed and bound in the U S A

(GIRLS IN TROUBLE was first produced by The Flea Theater (Jim Simpson, Artistic Director; Carol Ostrow, Producing Director), with the first performance on 12 February 2010. The cast and creative contributors were:

HUTCH .... Andy Gershenzon
TEDDY ....Brett Aresco
BARB/KIT ....Betsy Lippitt
SANDRA .... Akyiaa Wilson
CINDY/SUNNY/CYNTHIA...............................Eboni Booth
AMANDA ....Laurel Holland
ROBERT .... Marshall York

Director... Jim Simpson
Assistant director... Keola Simpson
Stage manager... Rachel Sterner
Set design.. John McDermott
Lighting design.. Zack Tinkelman
Costume design.. Amanda Bujak
Sound design..Jeremy Wilson
Puppet design... Campbell Ringel

CHARACTERS & SETTING

HUTCH, 22, *attractive, upper middle class college boy.*
TEDDY, 21, HUTCH's *buddy, naive about life but
  academically sharp.*
BARB, 22, *plain suburban college girl.*
SANDRA, 32-42, *white or African-American depending on*
  CYNDY-SUNNY-CYNTHIA.
CYNDY-SUNNY-CYNTHIA, 7, 27, *and* 47. SANDRA's
  *daughter. These roles are played by the same actress. She
  can be either African-American or white (see NOTES,
  following).*
AMANDA, 41, *confident, professional New York mother of*
  KIT, *and sharp-witted host of a T V and radio cooking
  show on P B S.*
KIT, 7, AMANDA *and* ROBERT's *petulant and political
  daughter.*
ROBERT, 40-50, *overbearing and self-assured hedge-fund
  manager,* AMANDA's *ex-husband and* KIT's *father.*

*A number of the roles may be doubled. For instance, the
actor who plays* HUTCH *or* TEDDY *may also play* ROBERT;
BARB *may play* AMANDA *or* KIT; SANDRA *may also play*
AMANDA *or* KIT.

ACT ONE *takes place in 1963*
ACT TWO *takes place in 1983*
ACT THREE *takes place in the present*

NOTES

The First and Second Acts are to be played together, with an intermission following the Second Act.

The style of the play is essential to define and is somewhat elusive because each Act has a different one. All acts are comedies—or at least are intended to have laughs—as well as horror shows. The frat-boy humor that initiates the First Act should wind up unexpectedly sensational; the Second Act shifts from the reality of the First to its own surreality; the Third becomes a high-style, almost Shavian verbal duel (though not without incident).

The sets for the three Acts are described as if each were for a full-length and realistic play. This is probably not possible and may not even be desirable. The director and designer are encouraged to imagine the play as they see fit.

The role of Cyndy-Sunny-Cynthia has been played successfully by both African-Americans and Caucasians. This version is written fo a black actor, but the dialogue need only be changed in three instances for a white. In Act One, when Cyndy says, "Sometimes I want to be white" (page 25); when played by a black actor she should say, "Sometimes I want to be black" when played by a white actor. In Sunny's monologue in Act Two, she refers to herself as a "nigger" if played by an African American and should be changed to "wigger" (a white person desperate to be black) if played by a white actor. In Act Three, Amanda says of Cynthia, "African American right wing pro-lifer?"; this should be changed to "Re-located cosmopolitan right wing pro-lifer?" if Cynthia is played by a white actress.

for A R Gurney
friend, shepherd, exemplar

ACT ONE

Scene 1

(A 1958 Cadillac pointed D S barrels north along I-71 in Ohio. Inside, HUTCH , twenty-two, and TEDDY, twenty-one, sit in the front, HUTCH driving. BARB, twenty-two, is in the back. Her head pops up for a moment so we can definitely see she's there, then passes out in the back. It is spring, 1963.)

HUTCH: So... I got another one for you.

TEDDY: Break it down...

HUTCH: Dirk Bogarde is invited to meet the Queen—

TEDDY: Dirk Bogarde?

HUTCH: The limey actor. He's invited to meet the Queen, but he's queer, so his agent needs to get a date for him. You know Diana Dors?

TEDDY: Ho, four bars beyond gorgeous. English Marilyn Monroe.

HUTCH: Right. Well, before she was Diana Dors, she was Diana Fluck.

TEDDY: Diana Fluck? That was her real name?

HUTCH: Yes! Jesus, Teddy, you're always so incredulous.

TEDDY: I am?

HUTCH: Yeah, you don't have to always not get *any*thing. So the agent sets up the date between Dirk

Bogarde and Diana Fluck, and the Mickey Mouse
was that Dirk has to introduce her to the Queen, and
he's sweating gator drops he's going to get her name
wrong. "It's Fluck, Fluck, there's an L in there" he
keeps saying to himself on the way over to pick her
up. They get to Buckingham Palace, and they're on
the receiving line, and Dirk's still nervous, "there's an
L, there's an L." And the Queen says, "Mr. Bogarde,
I've always enjoyed your movies, what a pleasure to
meet you," and he says, "Thank you ma'am, and your
majesty, please allow me to introduce my date, Diana
Clunt."

(A beat as TEDDY *gets it, laughs.* HUTCH *hits something in
the road.)*

TEDDY: You just hit something!

HUTCH: Doesn't mean squat.

TEDDY: Skunk, I think.

HUTCH: What's a skunk doing on I-71?

TEDDY: Leaving Cleveland. Just as we're heading in.
Doing 85, man...

HUTCH: We're late. Haven't even seen a sign for 90 yet.
Any fuzz?

TEDDY: Not at one A M going on two.

(After a moment:)

HUTCH: Teddy, she doesn't dig me at all!

TEDDY: You don't know that for sure.

HUTCH: Bite me, man. I've got radar for that shit.

TEDDY: I thought you were going to make her the
sweetheart of S A E.

HUTCH: I should've pinned her—I could've. But now
it's too late. At the beginning we couldn't stop talking
to each other. It was that laryngitic voice. Never heard

anything like it, couldn't get enough of that voice. Still can't.

TEDDY: She's the campus wet dream—Homecoming Queen shoe-in next year. Golden hair, saucer-blue eyes, perfect bod—

HUTCH: But at first it was that voice...

TEDDY: I don't think I saw you for a month.

HUTCH: We'd talk to each other so close, our mouths would practically be on top of each other, as if we were kissing and talking at the same time. Didn't need to kiss her, didn't want to kiss her, there wasn't time, we had so much to say. I couldn't get enough of her, she couldn't get enough of me, just kept talking, pouring ourselves into each other's brains and organs. When she'd breathe in, I'd talk, when I'd breathe in, she'd talk. She'd take out a weed, I'd go to light it for her, she'd cup my hand. Now that, Teddy boy, is one of the green lights you're always asking about. The sexiest thing a girl can do is hold your hand when you light her coffin nail, draw you to her. It's like fucking, just lighting her ciggie! She takes out the ciggie, you light the lighter, or a match, hold it halfway toward her so she has to take your hand, has to draw it to her. Lock her eyes, and if she does it slowly, from there it's a sure thing. So seductive, man. That's why we did it six, eight times on the first date!

TEDDY: You...you screwed her six or eight times on the first date?

HUTCH: No! Lit her cigarette! It was better than screwing. The agony of postponement. Sublime, *(French accent) anticipation terminale*. I held off as long as I could before kissing her...

TEDDY: How long was that?

HUTCH: Second date. Which was really just an extension of the first. I was with her till four seconds before she had to check in at Huffman that night, then showed up the next morning for breakfast. We went to the union, our mouths so close, babbling, I was telling her about Dad and D C, what it was like to hang out in the White House, how I wanted to go everywhere in the world first, go everywhere in the world with *her*. I practically asked her how she felt about being First Lady.

TEDDY: Yeah? After...twelve hours?

HUTCH: Oh, yeah, I'm telling you, Ace, this was real! And she was telling me how all she wanted was to get out of Granville, Ohio, with me, away from academia. She's never left it.

TEDDY: Never?

HUTCH: Well, she's been to Columbus. I think she had lunch once in Xenia. She loves her father, but Jesus, how constricted it is for her, all those poli-sci profs watching over her from the moment she was born. She thought D C was Paris, she wanted to go to D C spring break insteada Lauderdale, see where I was born—

TEDDY: Putty in your hands...

HUTCH: I'm tellin' you, man! Oh, baby! And we just split the union and got into this car—*this car*—and drove out the back entrance to Ebaugh's Pond, and it was all I could do to keep driving—

TEDDY: —sort of like now—

HUTCH: Ha ha! We're cool, we're cool, never had an accident in my life.

(HUTCH *deliberately swerves to freak* TEDDY. *Tires screech.*)

TEDDY: Hutch!

HUTCH: She was so close to me, her leg right up against mine, her hand on my thigh, talking right into my cheek while I was driving. And we stopped at Ebaugh's, I put the gear in Park, didn't even turn off the ignition, just turned my head and my mouth, sort of ran into hers, so suddenly we were kissing, and I thought I was going to pass out, no shit. I came in my pants like a teen-age cherry.

TEDDY: Know what people don't see in you? You're a genuine romantic. That's why you're such an ass-man.

HUTCH: I don't want to be an ass-man. Well, I don't want to be *thought of* as an ass-man, because then you can never be one.

TEDDY: Dig it.

HUTCH: It was so outta sight that night with her—I never once thought of the next step—never thought of anything but kissing her, just the way I hadn't even thought of kissing her but only of talking to her up till then. I mean you know me, every chick, I'm dying to put the make on as soon as I meet them, figuring out how to kiss them, and if I do get to kiss them, right away how to get to second base, and when I get to second, right away third. And—

TEDDY: How *do* you get to second base?

HUTCH: (*Indicating* BARB *in back seat*) She still out?

TEDDY: Yeah.

HUTCH: Four whiskey sours, she oughtta be. What usually works for me is: while kissing the girl, I caress the side of her cheek and then go into the natural flow of her neck and then as if it were all part of one graceful, completely unexceptional movement so she won't be alarmed, onto her breast. Nothing at all dramatic. You kill it if it's all neon and "Breast! Breast! I got her breast!" Treat it like a toe. And she'll realize, "Oh, this is okay, no big deal, like he's not on my *breast* or anything, my virtue's intact, and P.S. it feels good" and do that for awhile, and the second I'm there... think about moving my hand inside her shirt or up under her sweater, so it's not just second base but actual bare tit—

TEDDY: Wait a minute, is second base bare tit or covered tit?

HUTCH: Second base is covered tit. Bare tit is second base but with a big lead. So right away at second base I'm figuring out how to go from bare tit to the honey pot—

TEDDY: The honey pot! Man, how do you get there?

HUTCH: Same way. Make sure she's breathing hard, release her tit, slowly bring your hand down, very slowly, you're not doing anything, rest it on her knee or the thigh...everything you're doing's unimportant. You're kissing her and her neck and her ear lobe like a wild man so all her attention's there, maybe whispering in her ear, and if she's breathing hard, you wind up under her skirt—

TEDDY: What if she's not breathing hard?

HUTCH: You adjust her breathing. Tongue her gums, they love that for some reason. Then under her skirt if you can just flick her a couple of times before she knows you're doing it, she'll get wet and then wetter, and all she'll think is you're kissing her.

TEDDY: A stealth fuck!

HUTCH: Dig it!

TEDDY: I never get anywhere near there. I'm lucky if I get a couple of French kisses and then go home with blue balls.

HUTCH: Well, that's why they invented the standing dry hump.

TEDDY: How does that work exactly?

HUTCH: The one thing girls get on you is how much you want them. So if you hold her tight, kiss her, get what you can, then get off on her with a standing dry hump—or a lying down dry hump—she's got nothing on you. You're your own man again.

TEDDY: Man, you've like got this all figured out mathematically. You already think like a president. At least this president.

HUTCH: Did you know Jack got laid by two different boojum on his wedding day?

TEDDY: No.

HUTCH: Once by his wife after the wedding, once by somebody else I'm not at liberty to say who right before.

TEDDY: He did?

HUTCH: Man, invent the Peace Corps *and* get laid by two different women on your wedding day? Every day a stag flick. In comes Angie Dickinson, twenty minutes later she leaves all wobbly and smiley and he's sending forty thousand troops to Europe. In comes Marlene Dietrich, twenty minutes later out she goes with a secret glow, and he writes *"Ich bin ein Berliner."* Somehow I don't think Ike and Harry S had that kind of luck.

TEDDY: Or that kind of vision. Do you believe it?

(HUTCH *gives* TEDDY *a "duh" look.*)

TEDDY: Oh, well, yeah, I guess your Dad'd know. That was a mistake, you know.

HUTCH: What?

TEDDY: *"Ich bin ein Berliner." Ein Berliner* is a kind of doughnut. He said, "I'm a doughnut." If he'd left out the *"ein"*, he would have been all right.

HUTCH: I know, I know. Don't think Sorenson didn't take shit for *that* fuck-up. But Christ, he could even screw up the Bay of Pigs and still get laid every night.

TEDDY: Can't imagine any president's ever going to make that mistake again. Invade a country because the C I A tells you all the people're going to greet you with open arms...

HUTCH: Man, Jack is so pissed at the C I A.

TEDDY: Do you call him Jack like, to his face?

HUTCH: 'Course not. Call him "Mister President." Though behind his back we call him "Master President" because he's such a kid, and Kruschev wiped the floor with him. Can't do that when the Undersecretary's around—he thinks it's disrespectful.

TEDDY: Will he get re-elected?

HUTCH: Sure, unless he really fucks up. Girls all get clit-ons over him. The left loves him since he unionized the feds, and business likes him 'cause he lowered taxes. What's left?

TEDDY: What's your plan?

HUTCH: Outta the Navy in '68, run for senate till I get it, then for V P in '76, either get it or not, run for prez in '80 or '84.

TEDDY: No, I mean as president. What do you want to do?

HUTCH: Well, it's sort of a loose agenda. I have to get elected first. Maybe when I get outta the Navy, be ambassador to some place—like Belgium. Then senator, then V P, then prez. And get laid every night!

TEDDY: I don't see how you can get laid more than you already do. You already get more ass than Elvis. Than Rock Hudson! But you did eventually nail Golden Girl, right?

HUTCH: Well, eventually, yeah.

TEDDY: When?

HUTCH: Second date.

TEDDY: Second date? You're the only guy on campus who'd call the second date "eventually". I thought you came in your pants.

HUTCH: Thanks for reminding me. With her hand on my thigh, I recovered in about thirty seconds. That night and every night thereafter for a year. Sometimes two, three times.

TEDDY: That second date—was she wearing a garter belt?

HUTCH: Well, yeah. Why?

TEDDY: You always say how much you like garter belts.

HUTCH: I do, I do. They focus everything on that little patch of thigh between the top of the stocking and the R F F L.

TEDDY: R F F L?

HUTCH: Reason For Fucking Living. Stocking, thigh, R F F L, garter. Like a frame.

(HUTCH *takes his hands off the wheel to illustrate the frame, hits something in the road.*)

TEDDY: Hutch!

HUTCH: We're fine, we're fine! Never had an accident in my life.

TEDDY: That was a dog!

HUTCH: Well, what am I supposed to do? Dogs aren't supposed to come running out on the Interstate. I mean, it's not a person. Where the hell is 90?

TEDDY: What went wrong exactly?

HUTCH: With Dinah? She realized D C wasn't Paris and I wasn't J F K. I kept telling her she was gorgeous and sensual and could have anybody she wanted, and she began to believe it and started having everybody she wanted which included the entire Beta house and that asshole with the flat-top, Brumbaugh. Maybe I shouldda got *her* pregnant, too. But I'm gonna take one of her father's courses next semester—

TEDDY: —Professor Vaughan—

HUTCH: The History of Soviet Tractor Parts or something. Make a point of saying something brilliant in every class if I have to steal it from Walter Lippmann...or even Drew Pearson.

TEDDY: Get to her through her father? Might work.

HUTCH: And Michelle.

TEDDY: Her best friend? Didn't you go out with her?

HUTCH: Michelle? A little.

TEDDY: I hesitate to ask, but how far'd you get?

HUTCH: Oh, all the way. That was the whole point—so Michelle'd go back and tell Dinah how good I was and Dinah'd remember what she was missing and go back with me.

TEDDY: I don't know much about females, but from everything I've read, girls don't really like it when you fuck their best friends.

(HUTCH *hasn't considered this.*)

TEDDY: (*Indicating* BARB *in back seat*) Was she wearing a garter belt?

HUTCH: Yup. I do remember that.

TEDDY: I knew a girl once got herself in trouble.

HUTCH: Yeah? What happened?

TEDDY: Her par-eye sent her away to have the kid. Came back, guys all figured she was loose and set up a bunch of gang bangs. She was real popular for about two weeks, then got so badmouthed she went a little crazy. Wound up going to a psychiatrist. Why'd you do it?

HUTCH: I didn't knock her up on purpose!

TEDDY: Why'd you screw her? I mean, you didn't even know her.

HUTCH: I didn't screw her. I was screwing Dinah—it just happened to be Barb's body. Barb's got a really cool lower half of a body. Great ass, thighs, nice calves. Pretty good lips, kind of lazy eyes, like half asleep, dying to be shook up. We were so shit-faced up at the S A E house I thought she was gonna blow lunch. So I fixated on the parts that reminded me of Dinah.

TEDDY: Only it wasn't Dinah.

HUTCH: But it was. The fuck was Dinah, the aftermath was Barb. She's my whole life, Teddy!

(HUTCH *hits something in the road.*)

HUTCH: What was that?

TEDDY: A giraffe, I think. Slow down, man.

HUTCH: Can't. She's got her Econ final at eight. We gotta get there, get this done, get her into that exam.

TEDDY: Oh, right. Well try keeping it under a hundred and ninety, okay?

HUTCH: Hey, how much trouble could we get into for this?

TEDDY: I don't know. I think you're an accessory.

HUTCH: Jee-sus! That means jail!

TEDDY: Yeah, maybe.

HUTCH: But that means you're an accessory, too, right?

TEDDY: Yeah, but not as much of an accessory.

HUTCH: Man, it sure as hell better not be knitting needles—

TEDDY: No!

HUTCH: —that's all you read about, rusty knives, coat hangers—

TEDDY: Jesus, no! Lynnie's had three of them, never a problem.

HUTCH: Dig it, dig it.

TEDDY: So that was it? A great ass and you fucked her?

HUTCH: No, she's got great legs, too. She was really up for it, buddy. Those white panties came flying off—no fightback whatsoever, so don't look at me like that. She was already wet, Ace, really wet, and she was so hot to trot she didn't even take off her garter belt. We did it in the graveyard...I mean, she's just as much to blame for it as I am.

TEDDY: Not on the pill...?

HUTCH: I don't think she gets much action. I don't know why—she's got such a great bottom half of a body. But you do have to have a chin.

TEDDY: She's a nice girl.

HUTCH: Well...

TEDDY: Come on, Hutch, that's not her fault. Her par-eye talked her into that.

HUTCH: Man, I need the Navy so bad. I've got to start growing up! Girl in the back seat I just knocked up and I don't even remember what she looks like. What's the matter with me? (*After a moment*) I've got to get her back, Teddy!

(*Blackout*)

Scene 2

(*Lights up on*)

(*A living room in the low-rent section of Cleveland.* SANDRA, *37, enters.*)

SANDRA: Cyndy? Cyndy!

(*We hear giggles offstage.*)

SANDRA: Cyndy! Keep away from the kittens!

(SANDRA *pulls* CYNDY, *7 and wearing pajamas, onstage.*)

SANDRA: Come on, honey, I told you not to be with them now. You got to be in bed.

CYNDY: I know, momma, I was just goofin'.

SANDRA: Now come on, almost one o'clock, a seven-year old girl's supposed to be in bed. You can play with them in the morning.

CYNDY: They're sleeping, you know?

SANDRA: That's what kittens do when they just been born.

CYNDY: Can I take one to bed?

SANDRA: No, honey, no, they don't want to be away from they momma, and they momma don't want them away from her neither. And they make a mess of your bed.

CYNDY: Just one?

SANDRA: No, baby.

CYNDY: Where's Daddy?

SANDRA: Yer Daddy and me had a little argument. He drove off.

CYNDY: He drove off? Usually when you fight, it's you drives off.

SANDRA: I know, baby, but I got people coming.

CYNDY: At one in the morning?

SANDRA: Supposed to be here an hour ago. Only time they could make it.

CYNDY: How come you and Daddy got so many friends we only see once?

SANDRA: Life's like that sometimes. Now I want you to go to sleep, and just remember, keep your door closed like usual.

(CYNDY *and* SANDRA *exit together to* CYNDY's *room.*)

(*Blackout*)

Scene 3

(*Lights up on*)

(*The Cadillac.* BARB *pops up in the back seat, hysterical.*)

BARB: I'm not doing this! I'm not doing it! Stop the car!

HUTCH: We're on I-71!

BARB: Pull over! On the shoulder!

TEDDY: She's opening the door!

HUTCH: Jesus, Barb...

(HUTCH *slams on the brakes, the Caddy swerves and squeals to a stop on the Interstate shoulder.* BARB *jumps out.* HUTCH *runs after her.*)

BARB: I'm not doing this!

HUTCH: You gotta!

BARB: I'm not!

HUTCH: *(Puzzled)* What's the matter? I thought we agreed to everything.

BARB: I'm not doing it!

HUTCH: Why? What's happened?

BARB: Nothing's happened. I changed my mind. This is no good.

HUTCH: *(Working it out)* You're...you're going to have the baby?

BARB: Yes.

HUTCH: *(Reminding her)* Because I'm not marrying you and moving to New Jersey to work in your father's bank for ten thousand dollars a year, you know.

BARB: Why not? A good job. Great money.

HUTCH: No...it isn't.

BARB: Really good money—

HUTCH: You want me to live my whole life a completely different, boring way working in your father's bank for ten thousand dollars a year because of a sex accident?

BARB: It's a good job. Plainfield is great. We have theatre, music—

HUTCH: It was one time! One time, everybody shit-faced at the S A E house—

BARB: It was more than that to me.

HUTCH: I've got a whole life out there! So do you. The fucking nerve of you and your father trying to tell me how to live my life! For...for...this!

BARB: You like me a little, don't you?

HUTCH: *(Sensing her need)* Yes, yes, you're a very nice girl.

BARB: We could live a really nice life together. We just have to try.

HUTCH: No we couldn't. I don't even know you. Forced into it like this?

BARB: Well why did you make a pass at me?

HUTCH: Not because I wanted to wind up working in a bank...

BARB: Well, why?

HUTCH: You're a great girl, fun to talk to, attractive...

BARB: I am?

HUTCH: You need to know this: You've got a great ass and great calves.

BARB: That's it?

HUTCH: No, no, you're a very great girl, too.

BARB: Then I don't hear from you for three months.

HUTCH: I got busy. I was in love.

BARB: You told me that was all over!

HUTCH: It wasn't quite. It isn't even now.

BARB: First time I see you in three months, two nights ago, you practically rape me. Why?

HUTCH: You just told me you were pregnant and that I had to go work for your father's bank in New Jersey for ten thousand dollars a year! What did you expect me to do?

BARB: Not that. Lots of people wouldn't have practically raped the other person.

HUTCH: Yeah...yeah. I'm sorry. Not my shining moment. I was just so damn mad.

BARB: It wasn't really rape. It wasn't anywhere near rape really. Just...rough.

HUTCH: You were wet.

BARB: Not right away.

HUTCH: But pretty soon. There's a tiger in there. You need someone to let that cat out.

BARB: It wound up kind of cool. I tried to get rid of it, you know.

HUTCH: (*Coaxing her back to the car*) You told me.

BARB: Went horseback riding every day, took two vinegar baths every day. I even threw myself down the stairs.

HUTCH: You told me. We better get going—we're gonna be late.

BARB: I don't know—

HUTCH: It's completely safe. The girl who told me about it has had three abortions from this woman, and she's fine.

BARB: I don't know—

HUTCH: You and your father and your mother and your brother and your sister and the cats and dogs of Plainfield are not telling me how to live my life!

BARB: Calm down, baby.

(HUTCH *kisses* BARB, *then has his hands all over her. It turns steamy. He hoists her skirt up.*)

BARB: But the cars...this is an Interstate...

(HUTCH *un-clips her garters, yanks down her panties, unzips his pants...*)

BARB: This time not so rough...

(BARB *and* HUTCH *have urgent sex. Headlights of passing cars flash by.* TEDDY *watches and masturbates. All three finish together. They clean up and dress.* HUTCH *takes out his flask, waves it in front of* BARB, *now mollified. She drinks.)*

HUTCH: Now come on. We can talk about the future after this is over.

BARB: Okay.

HUTCH: Here.

(HUTCH *helps* BARB *back into car; she passes out.)*

HUTCH: It's really for the best. (*Shuts her door, gets behind the wheel. Amazed)* Jesus, what you have to do sometimes.

(HUTCH *floors it. The Caddy screeches off.)*

(Blackout)

Scene 4

(Lights up on)

(The porch outside SANDRA'*s house.)*

(Cats meow O S. CYNDY *enters from her bedroom, creeps toward the cats. Before she can get out the door—)*

SANDRA: *(O S)* Cyndy! Go back to bed and keep away from those kittens!

(CYNDY *freezes, caught. She runs back into her bedroom.)*

(Cross-fade to:)

Scene 5

(The nose of the Cadillac is parked outside SANDRA'*s house.* HUTCH, TEDDY, *and* BARB *approach* SANDRA'*s front door.* HUTCH *stops.)*

HUTCH: Oh. I need your half.

(BARB *slowly hands bills to* HUTCH.*)*

HUTCH: Fifty...one hundred...a hundred and twenty...

(HUTCH *waits for the rest, but* BARB *can't find it. She digs into her purse, pulls out one more bill, hands it to him.*)

HUTCH: A hundred and twenty-five. Thanks. Are you okay?

BARB: Yeah.

HUTCH: What?

BARB: Yeah.

HUTCH: Good, good. We're right here with you.

(HUTCH *rings the doorbell.* SANDRA *opens the door.*)

SANDRA: Come on in.

(HUTCH, TEDDY, *and* BARB *enter* SANDRA's *living room.*)

SANDRA: Which one of you—?

HUTCH: I'm Doug. This is Sharon. This is Lou.

SANDRA: Sit down, dear. Would you like some whiskey?

HUTCH: (*Impatiently*) She's had pretty much to drink already.

(SANDRA *slowly pours* BARB *a double.*)

SANDRA: A little more won't hurt.

(BARB *stands up, scared.*)

SANDRA: Sit down, dear.

(BARB *sits.*)

HUTCH: (*Pointing to his watch*) Aren't we—?

SANDRA: We got all the time in the world.

HUTCH: We don't know Cleveland, and once we got off 422 onto Ontario—

SANDRA: You could've asked somebody. Or are you scared of a colored neighborhood?

HUTCH: No! No!

TEDDY: No! No!

SANDRA: It's okay, dear, we got plenty of time. Now drink this on up as much as you can.

(BARB *drinks*.)

SANDRA: Mild night tonight, isn't it?

(BARB *gags*. HUTCH *is exasperated*.)

TEDDY: I thought you weren't supposed to drink when you're pregnant.

SANDRA: That's fine, that's enough. Let me take you upstairs.

(SANDRA *leads* BARB *upstairs. They exit.*)

HUTCH: You're not supposed to drink when you're pregnant if you want to have the baby, asshole!

TEDDY: Oh, right.

HUTCH: I don't see how she's going to get this done in time for Barb to take her Econ final. Almost three-thirty. She's so slow!

(*We hear strains of Johnny Mathis O S.*)

TEDDY: Maybe you shouldn't have gone to that party.

HUTCH: Fuck you in the heart.

TEDDY: Right. Well, as long as we're outta here by four-thirty, four-forty-five at the latest. I don't think it's a good idea to try and hurry her.

HUTCH: No, no, right.

(SANDRA *enters*.)

SANDRA: Where the fuck you boys been? It's three-thirty! Can't bring a girl in here with only one hour to go!

HUTCH: We don't know Cleveland—we drove around for more than an hour.

SANDRA: Why didn't you leave earlier? I ain't puttin' her in danger just 'cause you didn't give yourself enough time.

HUTCH: No, of course not. How's she doing?

SANDRA: I want her relaxed. I put on some Johnny Mathis.

TEDDY: Can't you give her something?

SANDRA: No—she's got to be awake enough to help. I gave her the only thing I could. Sorry if the whiskey's not up to university standards.

HUTCH: University standard is that it's brown and got alcohol. How...how do you do it?

SANDRA: Massage the uterus. Induce a miscarriage.

HUTCH: *(Suddenly queasy)* Oh.

SANDRA: Don't get sick on me now.

TEDDY: Where'd you learn this?

SANDRA: Korea. I was a nurse during the war.

TEDDY: Hunh. Is there anything we can do?

SANDRA: You've done enough. I need to collect my two hundred dollars.

TEDDY: Two hundred?

HUTCH: *(Handing her a wad)* Oh, sure. Better count it.

SANDRA: You wouldn't dare mess with me, Johnny. Or whatever your name is. Just wait here. *(She exits.)*

TEDDY: Two bills? Barb gave you a hundred and twenty-five!

HUTCH: There's gas...wear and tear on the car. We may stop at the Buckeye Diner on the way back. Good scrambies.

TEDDY: You're making a profit on this?

HUTCH: No! Not making a profit! She'll get it back if we don't need it. This is getting hairy.

TEDDY: Yeah, an hour's not much time. I hope she knows what she's doing.

HUTCH: Yeah, right. *(A moment, then...)* You really think I shouldn't've fucked Michelle?

(Blackout)

Scene 6

(Lights up on)

(SANDRA's living room, an hour later.)

TEDDY: Does the Undersecretary know about this?

HUTCH: Are you unborn? That's all he'd need—Kennedy'd get rid of him between forward and back in that rocking chair.

TEDDY: You think?

HUTCH: The son of the Undersecretary of Defense sent to jail for knocking up a chick? No, he doesn't know, and he's not going to. Massage the uterus...where is the uterus?

TEDDY: Right next to the ovary, I think. I threw myself down the stairs once.

HUTCH: Yeah, but that was to kill yourself, right?

TEDDY: Yeah.

HUTCH: Well...you're a lot more serious than I am. Than most people. You get a lot out of college I don't.

TEDDY: And vice-versa. I feel really bad for her.

HUTCH: Yeah, me too. You're a true friend to come along with me, Teddy.

TEDDY: I am? I thought I was just incredulous. Too incredulous to ever get laid.

HUTCH: You are, and a handjob. But I'd flip out if I had to deal with this on my own.

TEDDY: Negative perspiration.

HUTCH: I gotta get started in the Navy. Learn to fly a plane—make a man outta me. Why don't you come with me?

TEDDY: I'm an English major. I haven't had all that R O T C-y.

HUTCH: Navy might take English majors. Jesus, I need so much maturation! Know what's great?

TEDDY: What?

HUTCH: A panty girdle. It's all stiff when you're on the outside, like armadillo time, baby, but when you get inside, you feel this armor on the back of your hand and all the creamy assflesh on the front. And once you're in, you're sort of trapped. It's really hard for a girl to get your hand out of her panty girdle once you're in.

(CYNDY *enters, heads for the kittens.*)

HUTCH: Hey, little woman.

CYNDY: Hey.

TEDDY: Wanna shake?

CYNDY: Sure.

(CYNDY *goes to* HUTCH *and* TEDDY, *they shake hands.* CYNDY *hears* SANDRA *approaching.*)

CYNDY: (*Running offstage*) Don't tell momma!

HUTCH: Okay! Don't tell momma what?

(SANDRA *enters suddenly carrying sheets and heading for the back yard.* HUTCH *and* TEDDY *jump up.*)

HUTCH: What's going on?

SANDRA: Nothing. She's fine.

HUTCH: What—what are you doing?

SANDRA: Burning the sheets.

(SANDRA *exits.* CYNDY *enters with a kitten.*)

CYNDY: Lookit Ray.

HUTCH: Hey, Ray! You're cute.

TEDDY: Hey, Ray...

CYNDY: Just born three days ago. Named him after Ray Charles.

HUTCH: The colored singer?

CYNDY: And his brother Sam after Sam Cooke and his other brother Little after Little Richard. (*Ray bites her.*) Owww! Now don't you bite me, Ray Charles! (*She bops Ray.*)

TEDDY: Fierce jungle beast.

CYNDY: Did you see my momma?

HUTCH: She just went out that way with some...with some laundry.

CYNDY: Promise not to tell her?

HUTCH: Total promise. What's your name?

CYNDY: Cynthia Sunset Treece.

HUTCH: Sunset...?

CYNDY: You boys look nervous.

TEDDY: We do?

HUTCH: You know what your mother's doing up there?

CYNDY: 'Course I do. Momma does it to me all the time.

HUTCH: She does?

CYNDY: Momma makes girls feel better, even though sometimes they don't look it right away. Always makes me feel better. I know what goes on. Sometimes I want to be white.

HUTCH: Yeah?

CYNDY: Sometimes I want to be Miss Pearl Bailey. And sometimes I want to be Jacquelyn Bouvier Kennedy! Now don't tell Momma. *(She runs offstage.)*

HUTCH: Mell-o-drama.

(SANDRA enters.)

SANDRA: I'm going to bring Sharon down now. You take care of her.

HUTCH: We will. What should we do?

SANDRA: Just be kind to her, let her rest.

TEDDY: She's got an exam as soon as we get back. Will she be able to take it?

SANDRA: An exam? Man, you cats got some sense of timing. If she's strong, she can take it. Have her lay down on the way back.

(SANDRA exits. After a moment, she enters with BARB, who is pale and subdued.)

HUTCH: Are you okay?

BARB: *(Barely audible)* Yes.

(HUTCH leads BARB to the front door, then passes her off to TEDDY. TEDDY and BARB exit. HUTCH confronts SANDRA.)

HUTCH: Did it work?

SANDRA: Oh, yes.

HUTCH: What if something goes wrong?

SANDRA: Nothing will go wrong.

HUTCH: Well, but what's a sign of something going wrong, just so I know.

SANDRA: Excessive bleeding. She'll bleed a little, but her napkin will take care of that.

HUTCH: And what do I do if there's excessive bleeding?

SANDRA: Will you quit? Take her to a hospital and get the hell out of town.

HUTCH: Oh, thank you, Sandra, thank you, thank you, thank you!

SANDRA: You're welcome. Gimme a little sugar, honey.

HUTCH: Sugar?

(SANDRA *kisses a stunned* HUTCH. *They hold the kiss. Finally,* SANDRA *breaks it.*)

SANDRA: Next time, come a little early, stay a little late.

HUTCH: Yuh. Uh, thanks.

SANDRA: You better get going, swelldick.

(HUTCH *exits, flattered.*)

SANDRA: *(To herself)* Hurry back!

(Blackout)

Scene 7

(Lights up on)

(The Cadillac pointed D S. BARB *is awake but groggy in the back seat. It is 6 A M.)*

HUTCH: So...it wasn't really that bad?

BARB: No. Not that I want to do it again.

TEDDY: Cool.

HUTCH: What did she do to you exactly?

BARB: I don't know exactly. Put her hand up my cunt and rubbed.

TEDDY: Did it hurt?

BARB: Yeah. Felt...weird. Like a part of the body being touched that's never been touched before. Like if someone put her ball point pen deep inside your ear, way beyond where she's supposed to.

HUTCH: Well, at least you haven't lost your sense of humor.

BARB: You don't know me very well. I don't have much of a sense of humor.

HUTCH: Oh.

TEDDY: But you're all right.

BARB: Yeah. Thank you for asking, Teddy. You're all relieved, aren't you. And excited.

HUTCH: Don't know about excited. But relieved and glad that you're okay.

BARB: Excited because you dodged a bullet and can get back to your jerk-off lives.

(Cross-fade to:)

Scene 8

(CYNDY's bedroom)

(CYNDY plays with Ray, who bites her.)

CYNDY: Oww! Oww! Hey, you!

(CYNDY snaps Ray's neck. Ray pees. She stares at him for a moment, then drops Ray on the floor, yawns, and goes to sleep.)

(Cross-fade to:)

Scene 9

(Inside the Cadillac)

(It is 7:45 A M, and BARB, HUTCH, *and* TEDDY *have arrived on the Norman Rockwellian campus of Denison University. The boys are excited.* BARB *is depressed. All look sleepless.* HUTCH *switches off the engine.)*

HUTCH: Well, here we are. Think you can take the Econ final?

BARB: I have to, don't I.

HUTCH: Not bad—fifteen minutes till your exam.

*(*BARB *gets out of the car, revealing to the audience that the front and back of her skirt are covered with wet, sticky, bright blood. When she sees it, she shrieks to wake the dead:)*

BARB: AHHHHH! AHHHHH!

*(*HUTCH *and* TEDDY *recoil in horror, don't know what to do—)*

(Cross-fade from)

END OF ACT ONE

(To)

ACT TWO

*(B*ARB*'s scream blends into* C*YNDY's as)*

(Lights up on)

*(C*YNDY*'s bedroom. She removes her pajamas during the first two sentences of her speech, revealing that she's underdressed as twenty-seven year-old* S*UNNY. It is 1983.)*

S*UNNY: (Dressing into* S*UNNY)* Nooooo, you poppin' shit pompous, booty-ass braggin', tongue clickin', dick-down, chunky thigh big-ass, bounce like my ace toon coon! You can't treat me like this, you shit!

*(S*UNNY *[formerly Cyndy] X S C, speaks into a microphone at a cafe. The microphone is not used for volume but for tone. She wears a Walkman around her neck and plugged into her ears, referring to it whenever she hears a rap lyric.)*

S*UNNY: That first night, you club me, you bling me, you come on to me all

Rolly on my wrist
Champagne pourin' from your fist
Golden rubies on my mind
cause you talkin' so fine—

All sharp and spif, you ain't no bamma from Alabama,
I know what I'm seein'—

Pieced up,
Creased up,
Stayin' dressed
to impress

And talk in that club like you never met anyone like
me, Danny, treat me fine that first night, no sippin'
syrup for you, you too upmarket for that codeine and
cough outta Texas—

Sippin' on syrup 'cause I love to lean
High as fuck 'cause I'm puffin' green
And I got more amphetamines
Than Eckerd's or Walgreens

No cable round your neck, 45 malt breeze not good
enough for you, you buy me Chandon, then Dom
Perignon, woo, too good for me, Danny. I just a po'
little ghetto girl nigger born and bred, ain't played
'afore in your ballpark. But you, eyes all soulful, you
say, "Sunny, you special," you say, well lots say that,
"you special," and I know they after these bubbles, but
you, Danny, you say, "Sunny, you special to me. To
me!"

Then you represent hardcore, that voice low, no
fakin' the funk, no jive—you all up in decency, honor,
inherent nobility of all womanhood, woo! No hoes
and bitches for you, Danny, you murk anyone lay a
hand on your sainted sister, yo' momma greatest living
woman and whatnot. And you ain't on the corner
dealin' bounce—you a entrepreneur! Eee-lec- tronics!
And you not after a store, you after a chain, blow up
like Mister Radio Shack, here to Nanjingabing or some
such. You been watching President Ronald Reagan
on the glass—Ronald Reagan, geezer ain't even up to
disco yet—

(Singing) Disco, disco duck yeah—

—and you say he gives you inspiration, work yourself
up, and then give back—all Christian an' all. No one
ever move on me like that. And you say we gonna
have us a Lear jet plane. My eyes are rollin'! Boys I
know turn tranny tricks for a *car*—and you all ,"Plane,

plane, Lear jet plane, baby!" And then from out your
soft leather bag you give me a Walkman. A Walkman!
Nobody in my bricks got a Walkman. No warranty,
and I don't know if it fell off a truck, but it's cool, the
latest—can even jog with it. Like I'd ever jog.

And I swole up and look in your soft eyes. You all milk
dipped in butter, so smooth, and drip that sugar on
me, and now you sounding like Barry White, J-curls
all glistening, and my magenta soul just melt, and
right then decide, I'm havin' you, and touch your
big-ass thigh, and you got a bone big as a baseball bat
just like that! No doo-doo pants for you, you a diesel,
everything tight. So when I just touch you, you get a
bone. Felt good—power all wit' me. This a cold world,
Danny, and you heat me right up.

And a course I had you back in the bricks, be braining
you all night, don't you never sleep? Juiced till I had
no fluid left in my entire body! You off quick and
thick, but what's cool is, you on the bone again in two
minutes! Never saw anything like it from nobody—
and for sure no Christian!

Back when, dick was terrifyin'
But Donna taught me good
Then I lipped the hood—alla y'all hood
Started tasting good
Now I'm a dick bitch verifyin'!

Woo, you skeet down my throat, on my face, tween
my bubbles, I thought you gonna put that beast up my
nose! Where's that in the Bible? Oh, I knowed they do
it ALL back in the Bible days—they just don't write
it down. I mean, musta been nasty or where do those
commandments come from? Peeps doin' it!

So I talk to my wisdom, Donna, and I tell her, and
Donna say, "Sunny, when you finished with that man,
could I please have him?" But I wasn't finished. My

momma say you too good to be true, and so I let you
and let you, Danny, 'cause I was lovin' you.
One month, then three, most nights, and I'm just
deeper and deeper into you. You bring me something
every night like a guilty husband. Telephones, V C Rs,
boom box, a ten-ton microwave, a answering machine I
can't no way figure out. I got boxes of shit I never even
opened. And somethin' called a laptop, which is what,
huh, something 2001 maybe, but this is 1983! What was
this, this laptop?

But then it commences to begin. I can tell you not quite
there with me so much. Come by my dibs late now,
just come for a good brainin' and if I cook you that
rib-eye. You fade me, Danny. Two weeks I can't get
a nod—you diss me, Danny, treat me like dogfood.
You got the power now—when you don't give a shit is
when you got the power. Indifference always got the
power. Then a phone call, then a booty call, then two
more weeks, no nod.

Then I know: I embarrassin' you. "Sunny, you don't
have to talk street," you say, all Prince Charles or
somesuch, but you know I growed up in the hood,
same as you, and you think I don't wanna get out? I
could shake hands with Nancy Reagan and those two-
inch hips, I look good in red, I can get all high society
with the Empress of Japan and whatnot. But how'm'I
s'posed to do that? You take me there? But no, you
goin' all Upnose on me and wanna leave me behind.

Then I know you deep. *This* is all you after! All'a'y'all!
Just this! These! This jenny. This fat ass. This nappy
dugout. Body parts! Home slice gotta hit the kitten.
But you can get these motherfuckers anywhere, why
they hafta be mine? Why didn't you go after Donna's
or Elizabeth's, anybody's, or maybe you did—they
all interchangeable to you! Go give *them* a kid! I was
in love with you, Danny! And all the time you posin'

and perpin'. This wasn't no fifty-fifty love, this was a hundred to zero! Sometimes I am dumber than a doughnut.

Then what DOOO you know? Miss a month...miss another month...then what's His name, yo' Christian friend intervene.

Then he hit the seed
To some a good deed
And from out the sky
Hear a little cry
—Waa, Waa—
Life on the march!

And things take a little turn...and who's got the power now, dog? I do—women do. We got the law on our side. Y'all may have upper body strength, but we got the law. I din't know that till last week, I went to Mizzz Honeycutt, Esquire. She tell me, "Sunny, he touch a hair on your elbow, we nail him for assault. Look wrong at you—abuse! Disrespect you—harrassment!" Ho, I got more power now even than indifference. If I decide and me and me alone to have Danny Junior— and ho, it's all up to me—I could dee-stroy your life. For twenty-one years! You have to support this kid for twenty-one years if I tells you to, that's the law! Everything! Ha ha ha—you gonna pay for not lovin' me. You won't get to high profilin', Mister Radio Shack, you be lucky to be a salesdog at Radio Shack when you're fifty! Rich! Rich!

And so uh course you bust on the scene last night, and out comes Barry White again, all dripping sugar. Fool, you think I don't see through that? You know I could wreck your life for twenty-one years!

Only...you tell me...you want the kid! "It would give my life meaning, Sunny." Excuse *me*? How you'd love a little boy and then a little girl and then another little

girl and a coupla more boys and maybe another girl
to even it out. And how you'd take care of me as their
mother forever, I would never have nothing to worry
about. I start to melt again. but then I check and I axe
myself, "he jivin' me to get me to get rid of it?" But
no, you mean it! "I want to teach them music," you
say, "perch 'em on my shoulder." Only you forget one
thing. You forget to say you love *me* or could love *me.*
You supposed to love me first, then them. You gonna
use me like a cow to get what you want, no thought of
me. You maybe don't even like me at all!

So you know what? I'm gonna take this thing you say
you love most and show you where the power at now.
There is no fucking way little Danny Junior's coming
into this world to delight you, roll its eyes at you,
give your life a purpose where there was none except
Walkmans and V C Rs. You'll never get this—this is
mine to do with what I want, and I sure as hell don't
want it. I've got three goddam words for what you did
to me, Danny. A-BOR-SHUN. Shit, my momma used to
do abortions for a living right here in Cleveland when
it was illegal, nothin' to it, 'cept for that once. How
could you not love me? How could you not? I'd'a done
anything for you!

So go on, tell me once more how much it would mean
to you to have a little boy, walk him to school every
day, teach him basketballin' and the trom-fucking-
bone, read him stories at night. Here's the haps, Danny:
No! And you think I won't do it? I snaps cats' necks!

(Fade to black)

END OF ACT TWO

ACT THREE

(Black)

(We hear the introductory theme of N P R's All Things Considered. *The plummy voice of an announcer from N P R soothes and distresses.)*

RADIO HOSTESS: *(V O)* I'm Wellesley Saint Louis Saint Drem, and tonight on *All Things Considered* we'll look at just how awful the world is...why America made it that way...and the unmitigated success of apology in our foreign policy. But first, stay tuned for *The Virtuous Vegan,* with our favorite *chef de cuisine,* Amanda Stark.

(Lights up on AMANDA STARK's *kitchen on the Upper West Side of New York. It is flooded with light and is the state of the art workplace of a professional chef. Stage center is a cooking island replete with all the latest gadgets and knives, including a Thermomix [or any food processor] and an induction plate, on which a steel wok contains a bubbling and steamy soup. A housephone and a hard line phone are somewhere.)*

*(*AMANDA, *forty-one, and* CYNTHIA, *forty-seven—the grown up* SUNNY *from* ACT TWO—*are in mid-fight, screaming at each other and wielding chef's knives.)*

CYNTHIA: You're a murderer! A godless murderer!

AMANDA: The hell I am! You are! And I'm going to kill you!

CYNTHIA: And I'm going to kill you!

AMANDA: Why won't you give up?

CYNTHIA: Why won't you give up?

AMANDA: Okay, hold it.
(To audience) This is the story so far.
(To CYNTHIA*)* You, take off.

CYNTHIA: Unh-unh.

AMANDA: Go ahead. You'll get your moment in a second, to say the least—

CYNTHIA: Sez who?

AMANDA: You have my word as a journalist.

CYNTHIA: Ha!

AMANDA: As a woman.

CYNTHIA: That's even more suspect.

AMANDA: Go, go. Honest.

*(*CYNTHIA *exits.* AMANDA *puts down her knife.)*

AMANDA: *(To audience)* Yesterday afternoon I got hit by a bike messenger—you know, one of those thuggy whirling speed cretins with a suddenly-chic orange messenger bag so cocky he does wheelies on ice? Whack! Dislocated my hip. Hurt like the highest order of fuck. Wound up in the E R at Roosevelt hospital right around the corner peeing in a little cup and undergoing thirteen hundred other irrelevant tests you have to endure so you can't sue the hospital later when they leave the speculum inside you. Some doctor popped my hip back in—ahhh! passed out *again!*—and coming out of my fainting fog, he says to me, "Congratulations," and I haven't the slightest, so he says, "You don't know? You're twenty-five weeks pregnant!" My jaw drops to my clavicle, my eyes double in size. Pregnant? Twenty-five weeks? So it wasn't perimenopause after all. I mean, I've heard of teen-age girls who give birth without even knowing

they're pregnant, but they're usually four hundred
pounds or dirt poor...but me? I was so sure it was
perimenopause—Janet Adelman is going through
the same thing! Extra six pounds, mood swings like
Big Ben's pendulum—if Big Ben's got a pendulum—
explains my bursting into tears in the most important
meeting of my life in front of all those P B S suits. I've
had exactly one sexual encounter in the last six months
so completely forgettable I completely forgot it.

First thing I do when I get up off the E R floor is make
an appointment for an abortion, tomorrow at one P
M. And because I'm this sort of celebrity, oh all right,
enough phony self-deprecation, I hate it, don't you, but
it's so popular here on the Upper West Side. Okay, I'm
a *bona fide* celebrity. I guess a cooking show simulcast
on both N P R and P B S and foodies calling me the
not-for-profit Martha Stewart and all those blogging
Amandas begging to cook my recipe collection in
hopes the Ephron sisters will make a movie about
them...I guess that makes me a something-or-other.
So because I'm this oh, all right, whatever I am, I get
a phone call from this doctor saying she's an O B-G
Y N at Roosevelt and that she'd like to help ease my
way through the procedure, and since my gyno's
on some last ditch scuba vacation deciding whether
to drown himself or not because health care reform
may not let his kids go to college, she sounds like an
angel. Roosevelt has strategies for smuggling celebs
in and out because, as I don't need to tell you, there's
paparazzi at every elevator bank, and every nurse is
a potential stringer for *The National Enquirer*. Could I
drop by her office so she can fill me in on the procedure
and hold my hand? "Oh, Doctor Rense, my hip is so
killing me, I don't suppose you make house calls." I
say jokingly, and I'm so freaked first by this dislocated
hip and now by an astonishing pregnancy and even

more by this impending abortion— *(Bursting into tears)* —I start crying, I'm sorry, just the thought of having an abortion makes me cry. They're so traumatic. And this Doctor Rense says, "Well, I guess I could make an exception in this case," and I'm breathless. She sounds so understanding, and since I have to recipe-test a dish I call my Sri Lankan Surprise for my show anyway, I say, "Nothing special, but why don't you come by for dinner?" And so, thirty minutes ago, my hip killing me—after my daughter Kit, who's seven, goes around the corner to the drug store to pick up my painkiller—

(KIT, *seven, enters and places a bottle of Percocet on a table D R, then mimes speaking on the housephone.)*

AMANDA: —the doorman phones to ask if it's okay to send Doctor Cynthia Rense up, and I throw a few things into a wok for my Sri Lankan Surprise, which is a very veggie soupy version of a mallum, not a big deal, no *sous vide* or anything.
(She addresses the audience confidentially.)
Don't you really deep down hate bicycles? I used to love them—solution to traffic, no pollution, all virtuous goody-goody greenie groanies—but riders always go against traffic and run red lights, usually up on the sidewalk as if they were still in Vietnam. But call them on any of it, and they say you're a right-wing fossil fuelist.

(CYNTHIA *enters, takes* AMANDA's *blood pressure.)*

AMANDA: She seems affable, authoritative, takes my blood pressure to prove she's a doctor. We exchange pleasantries—
(To CYNTHIA) —and if you get mad at the bicyclists when they come at you in the night without a headlight they scream at you for restricting their free speech.

CYNTHIA: Free speech?

AMANDA: Yes, the right of every American to scare the
shit out of every other American. I used to think they
were all dreamy and poetic anarchists, but after that
guy hit-and-runned me, I know in their gut they're
bully boy fascists.

CYNTHIA: Well, you know what they say: a
conservative is a liberal who's been mugged.

AMANDA: Yes, and a liberal is a conservative who's had
an orgasm.
(To audience) And she flatters me—

CYNTHIA: *(To audience)* It wasn't flattery.
(To AMANDA) This is something I can tell my
grandchildren—I was invited to Amanda Stark's for
dinner!
(To audience) This was—
(To AMANDA) I watch *The Virtuous Vegan* every chance
I get, listen to it in the car—

AMANDA: So you're the one.

CYNTHIA: Don't give me that—your ratings are higher
than anything else on N P R or P B S. Every cable
channel's got a cooking show, but no radio does, and
you're the only one who sprinkles recipes with politics.

AMANDA: Well, you know public broadcasting.

CYNTHIA: I loved it when you had Bruce Willis on
making that cactus frittata and in the process got him
to reveal his right wingery. And then julienned him
like a cabbage.

AMANDA: I prefer to let them self-destruct. They
usually do.

CYNTHIA: And that weird guy from Alaska! Thought
every state should have its own currency—what was
he?

AMANDA: Libertarian. Often the unknowns are better guests than the superstars. The one person I regret never getting was William F Buckley. The one I can't get now is Christopher Hitchens.

CYNTHIA: He's probably scared of you. Does he cook?

AMANDA: He eats!

CYNTHIA: *(To audience)* Then she brings out all her abortion credentials—how her mother had been a crusader for a woman's right to choose and how her whole family ate and drank opposition to the war in Vietnam breakfast, lunch, and dinner. Then she starts tearing up. "I hate abortions," she says, but they all say that.
(To AMANDA*)* My mother was an abortionist.

AMANDA: Yow.

CYNTHIA: Back in Cleveland, when it was illegal. She learned how to do it as a nurse in the Korean War. Nine hundred and one successful abortions, never a problem till the nine hundred and second.

AMANDA: What happened?

CYNTHIA: Couple of rich-kid college kids came into the house two hours late one night, she had to work too fast. The girl almost bled to death on the way to the hospital. She told them Momma's name, Momma spent three years in jail.

AMANDA: It was a terrible time.

CYNTHIA: That was only half the hell. I tracked down the girl later—she never could have children. The boy who did her had a big political future but was killed on the *S S Kitty Hawk*, an aircraft carrier, during Vietnam. *Roe versus Wade* put Momma out of business.

AMANDA: Thank God.

CYNTHIA: Depends on your perspective.

AMANDA: *(To audience)* And I thought I was credentialled. I asked her if she'd like something to drink—a little '04 Corton-Charlemagne, my usual, then—

(CYNTHIA *gives* AMANDA *a wrapped box.)*

AMANDA: *(To* CYNTHIA*)* My goodness—a present? House calls and presents? What medical school did you go to and how do I get my daughter in?
(To audience) But before I can open it, my soon-to-be-but-not-soon-enough-for-me ex-husband shows up—

(ROBERT *enters, grabs jar of pills.)*

AMANDA: *(Still to audience)* —for his once-a-week phony love fest with our daughter Kit. As usual, we have a screaming fight.

ROBERT: Percocet—the Jerry Lewis drug! Jesus Christ, Amanda, you let Kit go into the streets to get your drugs by herself? She's seven!

(KIT *enters.)*

AMANDA: *(To* ROBERT*)* The drugstore is fifty yards away on Columbus—it took two minutes.

ROBERT: Why were they so important you couldn't get them yourself?

AMANDA: I've got a dislocated hip! That's what the meds are for!

ROBERT: Percocet's a fucking narc!

AMANDA: I know that, Robert—

ROBERT: You better not be thinking of giving them to her!

AMANDA: What!

ROBERT: You said she's had trouble sleeping since I left.

AMANDA: She has, and when she comes into my room crying at two A M, I—not you, not her father,

her mother—I put her next to me in bed and talk her to sleep. Even when she's inconsolable it has never once occurred to me to give her controlled substances, or pour her a Johnnie Walker Blue, or hit her with a mallet! Just you!

ROBERT: You think this is funny?

KIT: Daddy—

ROBERT: You're sending our daughter out for your drugs? You are fucking irresponsible, Amanda!

KIT: Are you endangering me, Mommy?

AMANDA: No dear. Daddy's just exercising his righteous indignation—impotently as usual. Now isn't it time for your nice dinner at Teodora across town and for the taller of the two of you to order the poison pasta?

(ROBERT and KIT exit.)

AMANDA: *(To audience)* How could I ever have found a guy who travels with his own personal mirror and a set of women's barbells attractive? Oh, and he didn't leave me. I kicked his petulant and hairless heinie out. *(To CYNTHIA)* I'm sorry you had to see that. Do you like habanero peppers?

CYNTHIA: Yes...

AMANDA: Some people can't tolerate them. Too hot.

CYNTHIA: I love a good cry.

AMANDA: Have to use them sparingly or they cover up the flavor of everything else.

CYNTHIA: They're not especially good for expectant mothers.

AMANDA: Fortunately, I hope to be a disexpectant mother tomorrow at one P M, thanks to you.

(To audience) And then it started to get weird.
(To CYNTHIA*)* Oh, your prezzie.

CYNTHIA: It's not really a prezzie, I don't want to misrepresent—

*(*AMANDA *opens the box, reveals two dead birds.)*

AMANDA: These are...?

CYNTHIA: Ptarmigan. A kind of grouse.

AMANDA: Ptarmigan. Where did you get them?

CYNTHIA: Oh, I shot them.

AMANDA: You shot them...how?

CYNTHIA: 12-gauge Winchester Parker reproduction with, get this, a twenty-six-inch barrel. I know you're a vegan, a famous vegan, but I really like meat, so I pretty much brought them for me.
(To audience) I had to shake her complacency somehow.

AMANDA: Well, they're...rivetting.

CYNTHIA: *(To* AMANDA*)* You can cook the broth, remove your portion, then cook mine with the ptarmigan.

AMANDA: I don't think they'll fit in the wok.

CYNTHIA: Oh, of course.

*(*CYNTHIA *violently chops their heads and feet off.* AMANDA *starts to faint.)*

CYNTHIA: Will they fit now?

AMANDA: *(To audience)* The room started spinning...
(To CYNTHIA*)* Yes...I suppose they will.

CYNTHIA: Oh, I'm sorry. How insensitive of me. Are you all right?

AMANDA: *(Rubbing her neck)* Yes...just need to get the blood circulating a little. The poor things!

CYNTHIA: I am so sorry...of course, you were empathizing with the ptarmigan, weren't you, the poor things...

AMANDA: Yes, I guess I was.

CYNTHIA: *(To audience)* She is so above us all, isn't she? *(To* AMANDA*)* We call that anthropomorphizing.

AMANDA: Yes...

CYNTHIA: But those are just game birds. Now you take someone who really suffers—a boy in Lake Charles, Louisiana, maybe, who's fly-fishing and by mistake catches the hook in the cornea of his eyeball—ooo, we can both anthropomorphize about that can't we, Amanda? Or that old lady in Truckee, Nevada, whose anesthetic failed and was conscious but unable to speak during the nine-hour bone marrow transplant in her leg—can you anthropomorphize with that, Amanda? I sure can. Or, *or* the twenty-five week old fetus in New York, New York, sucked from its mother's uterus after the painful scrunching of all its bones including the skull so that the brains can be pulled out by the polyp forceps and then suctioned out with a catheter under a pressure of fifty-five millimeters of mercury so that all that's left are the spicula, you know, the shards of bone. You can feel the anthropomorphosis of that agony, can't you, Amanda, or does the assassination of a living fetus just not stir your blood as much as the decapitation and pedal amputation of two already dead ptarmigan? The...poor...things?

AMANDA: *(To audience)* What was this? *(To* CYNTHIA*)* Who are you?

CYNTHIA: Just someone who believes that the innocent should be allowed to live.

AMANDA: *(To audience)* Oh my God, one of them. Get my ass to the house phone!

(AMANDA *moves for the house phone,* CYNTHIA *blocks her.*)

CYNTHIA: Don't.

AMANDA: I told her to get the hell out. She kept telling me not to be afraid.
(To CYNTHIA*)* Get out get out get out!

CYNTHIA: Don't be afraid, don't be afraid, don't be afraid!
(To audience) I had to defuse her fright, prove to her I wasn't here to steal her silver or harm her in any way, but she panicked, so— *(She empties her purse and pockets to show she's carrying no weapons.)*

AMANDA: What're you doing?

CYNTHIA: See? Nothing in here—

AMANDA: What—?

*(*CYNTHIA *takes off all her clothes.)*

CYNTHIA: Oh, you poor thing. I'd feel exactly the same way. Of course you're frightened, Amanda. Who wouldn't be? You need reassurance. I mean, a stranger comes into your apartment, pretends to be your gynecologist, what a betrayal of trust!, witnesses the way you interact with your volatile husband and pretty angry daughter, though understandably angry, whoo, lots going on there—

AMANDA: Wait, stop!

CYNTHIA: —almost makes you faint by chopping off game birds' heads and feet—yeww—I'd feel exactly the same way, Amanda—what if I'm carrying a concealed weapon? But I'm not. See— *(She removes her bra.)* Nothing here— *(Spinning)* —nothing here—

AMANDA: Put your clothes back on!

CYNTHIA: You need to know I'm not armed. You can strip search me. Deep cavity if you want. I'm not a violent person—don't be afraid of me.

AMANDA: *(To audience)* I was totally afraid of her.
(To CYNTHIA*)* I'm totally afraid of you! You're nuts!

CYNTHIA: Not only not nuts, not armed. See? Want more proof?

AMANDA: No!
(To audience) Though I can't for the life of me imagine what that would be. I didn't care if she was unarmed, she was out of her mind, and I told her I was calling the doorman to get the cops.

(CYNTHIA *steps aside.*)

CYNTHIA: Go ahead.

(AMANDA *heads for the phone.*)

CYNTHIA: But I thought progressives were supposed to be so open to new ideas.

AMANDA: *(On phone)* Carvalho?

CYNTHIA: Of course most progressives are really closet re-gressives, fuddy duddy regulationists who worship Europe.

AMANDA: *(To audience)* Hmmm?

CYNTHIA: You've really got nothing to be afraid of physically, you certainly can't be afraid of anything I might say—you chop up and eat people like me five times a week, you want to go toe to toe with Christopher Hitchens.

AMANDA: A little bell went off, then a siren. Could she possibly be a guest? African-American right wing pro-lifer? How many of those do you get in one lifetime?

CYNTHIA: *(To audience)* She thinks I want to be on her show—

AMANDA: *(To audience)* I've had lots of weird auditions—woman sneaking up under my umbrella in the rain...once in an elevator in Chicago a guy got us stuck between floors so he could sing me the song he wrote for Hillary's campaign. But nobody with these balls. Impersonating a gynecologist to get into my apartment and taking off all her clothes to prove she hasn't got a gun? Those are firsts!

(CYNTHIA *sits, is completely comfortable naked in* AMANDA's *home.*)

CYNTHIA: *(To* AMANDA*)* Who knows? You might even change my mind.

AMANDA: *(To* CYNTHIA*)* I don't want to change your mind. I don't care about your mind.

CYNTHIA: Oh come on, everybody in this town would like one less right wing pro-lifer.

AMANDA: No, eight is just the right number.
(To audience) She was right—what did I have to fear from her? I do chop up and eat people like her five days a week. But she was going to have to work for it. We don't give these guest slots away- particularly to unknowns. *(On phone)* Sorry, Carvalho. I...I may need you later...just not right now.
(To CYNTHIA*)* Tell you what. Put your clothes on, don't get between me and my housephone, and I'll let you rant for ten minutes.

CYNTHIA: *(To audience)* Bingoringo!
(To AMANDA*)* Deal. And dinner?

AMANDA: I don't think I can cook ptarmigan that fast.

CYNTHIA: Sure you can. *(She dresses.)*

AMANDA: We'll see. Tell me, do many women carry firearms in their vaginas? Of course most men think I do. You're quite the little actor, you know?

CYNTHIA: It's okay, you can say "actress" —I'm a girl. Only acting I've ever done was outside an abortion clinic in Jackson, Mississippi.

AMANDA: What part did you play?

CYNTHIA: The fetus.

AMANDA: The fetus.

CYNTHIA: Want to hear some of my lines?

AMANDA: Absolutely.

(AMANDA *is rivetted. She drinks wine continuously.*
CYNTHIA *doesn't drink at all.*)

CYNTHIA: As the mother'd enter the clinic grounds,
I'd follow her outside the fence, as the law requires.
(Imitating fetus) "Please let me come out, Mommy.
It's so dark in here, I want so badly to go on a picnic
with you and Daddy, braid my hair, do you think I'd
look good in a ballerina dress? Please don't murder
me, Mommy or I'll never taste ice cream or laugh
with other boys and girls on their birthdays. Please,
Mommy, please let me see the sun, don't murder me..."

AMANDA: My God, how nouveau Goth. You sound as
though you've been in many birth canals.

CYNTHIA: Pregnancy is my profession.

AMANDA: Did your fetus impression in Alabama work?

CYNTHIA: Mississippi.

AMANDA: Same thing.

CYNTHIA: No, it isn't, metropolitan provincial.
Alabama's got fourteen abortion clinics left.
Mississippi's only got one.

AMANDA: Well, did you convince anyone in
Mississippi?

CYNTHIA: Sixteen out of twenty.

AMANDA: You are scary.
(To audience) She's a gift.

CYNTHIA: You probably think this is scary: I've got six kids—twelve adorable little carbon footprints—and I wasn't going to have any.

AMANDA: Six? Why so many?

CYNTHIA: I want to make sure my kind of person outnumbers yours.

AMANDA: Ah, a reverse racial profilist.

CYNTHIA: Nothing to do with race—I'm talking about belief systems. I had my first one at twenty-seven. Freshman in college.

AMANDA: *(To audience)* At twenty-seven, I was a beeraholic nymphomaniac. I loved the Reagan years. Oh, not politically, of course. Extracurricularly. At twenty-eight I had my first radio show. And my first three-fourths of an orgasm.

CYNTHIA: I was going to abort the first one, who turned out to be little Jordan. Twenty years ago. But my husband Danny convinced me otherwise. You know how?

AMANDA: *(To CYNTHIA)* By bursting into your house and giving you a deep cavity search?

CYNTHIA: You got it. *(To audience)* But not in the way you think.

AMANDA: You were a freshman at twenty-seven?

CYNTHIA: *(To AMANDA)* Yup. Danny and I come from places you only see on T V when there's a riot going on. I was blowing my whole life. Danny convinced me we could change our lives—just as you can, just as we all can, through love. I went to rehab, learned to talk like you, re-invented myself—this is America after all—helped Danny become the electronics mogul he wanted to be. Bigger than Radio Shack.

AMANDA: Bigger than Radio Shack?

CYNTHIA: Danny's sole owner of H T I.

AMANDA: Home Theatres International? My God, there's one on every block—I get all my T Vs at H T I.

CYNTHIA: Well, don't stop now—I can get you a price. So had my little softball Jordan, then Miriam and Noah before I even got my B S in bio. Had Isaiah, Magdalene—we call her Maggie—and got pregnant with Ruth at med school.

AMANDA: So you are a doctor?

CYNTHIA: No, quit after two years. Too many wonderful kids and a purpose in life that transcends medicine. Be easier on you and your little girl if she had a sister. It's not fair to her that you force her to be an only child.

AMANDA: I didn't force her—

CYNTHIA: You're forcing her right now.

AMANDA: It's admirable you love being a mother, but I don't love being a mother, at least not of more than one, and besides, this whole procedure is over in fifteen minutes.

CYNTHIA: Oh, really? Let me kill you the same way— and then you can say, "Oh, smashing my skull and squashing my intestines wasn't so bad—it was over in fifteen minutes."

(AMANDA *stops. This is more difficult than she thought.*)

AMANDA: How did you get my name?

CYNTHIA: Oh, we know everyone who's having an abortion.

AMANDA: You know everyone who's having an abortion? Like...in the world?

CYNTHIA: In whatever area we focus on. It's about as hard to get hospital records as it is to steal an identity on the Internet.

AMANDA: Who's "we"?

CYNTHIA: A bunch of us.

AMANDA: Funded by trillionaire Danny?

CYNTHIA: Some.

AMANDA: So, a well-financed seeky-seeky naked right-to-life collective hopscotching the nation for whispers of potential babylets. Do you wear hoods?

CYNTHIA: No. How's your hip? Does it hurt?

AMANDA: Only when it hears things that scare the shit out of it. Tell me about your group.

CYNTHIA: Maybe later. After the habaneros.

AMANDA: Do people often let you into their homes?

CYNTHIA: All the time.

AMANDA: Why?

CYNTHIA: Same reason you did. They think they're smarter and they have the morally superior argument.

AMANDA: They're right.

CYNTHIA: See?

(A beat)

AMANDA: Do you always take your clothes off?

CYNTHIA: I do whatever it takes.

(AMANDA sings a few notes of the Twilight Zone theme.)

AMANDA: What's your success rate?

CYNTHIA: You wouldn't believe it.

AMANDA: Try me.

CYNTHIA: One hundred percent.

AMANDA: You get every single woman to agree to have their babies?

CYNTHIA: Something like that.

AMANDA: *(To audience)* Does Homeland Security know about this babe? How many of them were there—two? Two million?

CYNTHIA: It's murder!

AMANDA: *(To* CYNTHIA*)* No it isn't! What's murder is what you do when you force fifteen-year old girls living in projects to suffer lives they don't want. Not to mention what you do to the unwanted baby.

CYNTHIA: *(To audience)* This is her best shot? Of course—she's on P B S.
(To AMANDA*)* You're just talking metaphorical murder, and besides, you're not fifteen, and if this— *(Indicating lavish apartment)* —is a project, put me on the dole. What we do is protect people from committing real murder.

AMANDA: The bottom line is, girls and women are going to have abortions. Now you want them clean and safe or rusty and dangerous?

CYNTHIA: That is not the bottom line—

AMANDA: Have you read *Freakonomics*?

CYNTHIA: Yes.

AMANDA: An increase in abortion leads to a decrease in crime.

CYNTHIA: You can't go around murdering babies just 'cause some of them might turn out to be criminals. You'd have your beloved A C L U in your underpants before breakfast.

AMANDA: *(To audience)* Wait a minute, wait a minute— *(To* CYNTHIA*)* It's not murder!

CYNTHIA: That little girl inside you's been alive ever since conception.

AMANDA: It wasn't a conception. It was a misconception. And let's keep this theoretical if you don't mind.

CYNTHIA: Why?

AMANDA: What's going on with me is personal and none of your business.

CYNTHIA: *(To audience)* Typical Lefty—keep it theoretical. "Do as I say but don't ever never ever question what I do."
(To AMANDA*)* The life or death of a baby girl is exactly my business.

AMANDA: *(To audience)* Typical right wing fascist— thinks hypocrisy negates all argument.
(To CYNTHIA*)* What makes you so sure it's a girl?

CYNTHIA: Just know. Little Amanda Junior. What's your hunch—boy or girl?

AMANDA: My hunch is it's neither—or it won't be as soon as you leave and I can call Roosevelt for a real doctor. And that's absurd about conception. You might as well say it was really a human being when it was just a feisty sperm swimming upstream, battling its little Olympic heart out for my suddenly-coveted uterus.

CYNTHIA: No, sperm on its own isn't life. It's the merge, and the chromosomes merged in little Amanda Junior fifteen minutes after orgasm—his, not yours, unless it was simultaneous. Did you even have one?

AMANDA: That's none of your business!

CYNTHIA: I'm so sorry—maybe I can help.

AMANDA: I did fine, thanks.

CYNTHIA: *(To audience)* Haw haw, I bet not.
(To AMANDA*)* Excellent! That means she's a true love child. Cells started multiplying only two hours after your explosive, mutually satisfying orgasm. She had a heartbeat just eighteen days after you hooked up, about the same time her eyes started to develop, and her spinal cord and nervous system appeared about three days after that.

AMANDA: *(To audience)* She's like a one-woman swarm of bats—except bats are cool. Viewers will galvanize against her. You're against her, right?
(To CYNTHIA*)* It's not a human being. In this country we don't treat a fetus like a human being.

CYNTHIA: I do.

AMANDA: Well, you shouldn't. We don't have funerals for miscarriages, we don't charge women who smoke dope or go skiing while pregnant with reckless endangerment.

CYNTHIA: Amanda Junior's brain waves could be measured after only forty days—and if someone is legally dead when there are no brain waves, makes sense they're legally alive when there *are* brain waves, right? Forty days!

AMANDA: Where do you get all these unprovable factoids?

CYNTHIA: Let me at your Internet, I'll show you.

AMANDA: Oh, you can prove anything on the Internet. I can prove the Red Sox blew up the World Trade Center on the Internet.

CYNTHIA: She'll have a lot of your inflections when she talks, Amanda. She can hear everything we're saying right now! Just think—she can hear her own fate being decided. She can hear you considering changing your mind, and she's so grateful you waited till now, Amanda!

AMANDA: *(To audience)* My viewers will love her—their blood will boil!
(To CYNTHIA*)* Look, you champion capital punishment, right?

CYNTHIA: You betcha!

AMANDA: And a just war, whatever that is.

CYNTHIA: Yup.

AMANDA: Now those're murder. You can't possibly reconcile killing living, fully formed humans but defend a drop of protoplasm that isn't even alive!

CYNTHIA: But it is alive—weren't you listening?

AMANDA: Oh, for God's sake, a fetus is alive the way an amoeba is alive, or an oyster or caviar. You can't wriggle out of it by saying an African-American on death row or an innocent housewife in Kabul should be whacked but a lump of Caspian Osetra shouldn't be!

CYNTHIA: Who's wriggling? The creep on death row has been proved guilty of murder, usually heinous, and the woman in Afghanistan is the accidental result of a decision made by the government of the people.

AMANDA: Then impeach the government.

CYNTHIA: And the judiciary?

AMANDA: Impeach them, too!

CYNTHIA: Little Amanda Junior is guilty of nothing.

AMANDA: Quit calling it Amanda Junior!

CYNTHIA: Okay, he or she lump of caviar has done nothing wrong. The guy on death row is not only guilty, he's had a whole trial and two billion appeals, with a defense attorney and a bushel of lawyers standing up for him, and still been voted guilty by twelve jurors and sentenced to death by a damn judge.

AMANDA: Oh, and what's your solution? Place every fetus on trial ? So a jury of its peers and a judge can decide which ones deserve to be aborted?

CYNTHIA: Be a hell of a lot fairer than it is now, where there's only one judge—you—and no jury! Amanda Junior has no lawyers on her side. You people have murdered more human beings in the history of the world than Stalin, Mao, Hitler, Pol Pot and Saddam Hussein put together. More than the bubonic plague— and innocent little boys and girls—

AMANDA: Oh, fuck Pol Pot! This is my choice— not yours or anybody else's! I'm not telling you or anybody else what to do with your fetuses, and I'm not about to let you or anyone else tell me what to do with mine!

CYNTHIA: *(To audience)* Now she's engaged. Always happens when you make it personal instead of theoretical. "Oh, but communism's intentions are so *compassionate.*" Yeah, on paper.

AMANDA: *(To audience)* Listen to her—trying to make a statistic out of an anecdote.
(To CYNTHIA*)* No pro-choicer runs around the country naked or otherwise forcing women to get abortions. Nobody on our side runs around killing people who disagree with us.

CYNTHIA: *(To* AMANDA*)* Nobody on our side does either.

AMANDA: What do you call the creep who killed Doctor Tiller? "Committed"?

CYNTHIA: No, we call him a murderer—just the way the jury did. What do you call the creep who killed James Pouillon?

AMANDA: Who's that?

CYNTHIA: Anti-abortionist shot for his convictions outside a school in Michigan.

AMANDA: Oh. Uh...

CYNTHIA: Somehow we don't hear much about him, do we? Could it be the press just doesn't like that story but loves Doctor Tiller?

AMANDA: The bottom line is, nobody's pushing abortions. We're not pro abortion, we're pro-choice!

CYNTHIA: Yeah, but it isn't just choice like which shirt should I buy—it's the choice of who lives and who dies.

AMANDA: Damn right—and I choose life. Mine. This is my body!

CYNTHIA: That is so narcissistic! *(To audience)* Isn't she so narcissistic?
(To AMANDA*)* Try and look at the bigger picture. Amanda Junior is part of your body for only nine months—

AMANDA: *Only* nine months—

CYNTHIA: You live to be ninety, your daughter lives to be a hunded and ten, nine months is a speck of sand in the scheme of things—

AMANDA: I don't want anyone telling me what to do for nine months or for a speck of sand!

CYNTHIA: After six of them, I know about pregnancy. Some are difficult, some are thrilling, but most are just an annoyance. You're not being asked to endure nine months of water-boarding—it's an inconvenience! What is five minutes out of your whole life compared to a hundred and ten years of another human being? She could be Alberta Einstein!

AMANDA: She could also be Newtonia Gingrich! It's my choice!

CYNTHIA: It is not! It's His.

AMANDA: *(To audience)* I thought I saw the star of Bethlehem over her head. *(Shaking her fist)* I'd like to lay *her* in a manger.
(To CYNTHIA*)* Oh, so you believe life isn't just chemicals.

CYNTHIA: Hey, I think life is chemicals, but that there's a head chemist.

AMANDA: Let me guess: You're a Christian.

CYNTHIA: That doesn't automatically make me ridiculous, I warn you.

AMANDA: I'm sure it doesn't— *(To audience)* —but we love you on T V.
(To CYNTHIA*)* You do believe He rose from the dead, sitteth on the right hand of God the father blah blah blah—

CYNTHIA: Of course! Without that, he's just another nifty philosopher.

AMANDA: And you admire all those Christian heavyweights—Thomas Aquinas, Jerome, Saint Augustine—

CYNTHIA: They guide my life—

AMANDA: Then how do you reconcile that they all considered a fetus a vegetative soul with the moral status of a plant? That if it continues to grow, it develops into nothing more than an animal soul? The collective wisdom of the Christian tradition bases fetal development on *delayed ensoulment*, so if you abort you're ending a life but not a person?

CYNTHIA: So...bought a book?

AMANDA: Yes, it's called The Bible.

CYNTHIA: Oh, that's just to avoid being a stereotype.

AMANDA: I read the entire Bible and all the works of Paul F.M. Zahl just to avoid being a stereotype?

CYNTHIA: Some people will do anything.

AMANDA: *(To audience)* Oooo, I gotta get her, gotta get her, gotta get her!

CYNTHIA: *(To audience)* Her mouth is watering so bad she can taste me!

AMANDA: *(To CYNTHIA)* So what about all that Aquinas and Augustine?

CYNTHIA: *(To AMANDA)* They didn't have the knowledge we have of advanced embryology.

AMANDA: So you don't completely blind yourself to science.

CYNTHIA: I love science! The flexible art. But you really only like it when it agrees with you. The moment your science is proved wrong, suddenly it's all creationist voodoo.

AMANDA: What science has been proved wrong?

CYNTHIA: I seem to have lost my papers proving global warming in last year's blizzard—

AMANDA: Stick to the point—

CYNTHIA: The sonogram. We didn't have access to 'em before *Roe v Wade* so we let you get away with "It isn't alive, it doesn't suffer." Until mothers saw the sonogram, we couldn't see the agony Amanda Junior would go through if she's aborted, mothers didn't know their little Jordans and Amanda Juniors'd feel such excruciating pain and horror, didn't know they sucked their thumbs, laughed and cried. But then along came *The Silent Scream*, and now there's high def sonograms to drive it home, and yet somehow all of a sudden, science doesn't matter. All that really matters is "it's the woman's right to choose." It's not.

AMANDA: It's the law!

CYNTHIA: It shouldn't be! Have you had the sonogram, the ultrasound, Amanda?

AMANDA: No, but I bet you and your Royal Shakespeare Company of Fetus Impersonators want me to.

CYNTHIA: We do.

AMANDA: Sure, get the mother bonding—that's why I haven't had one.

CYNTHIA: Aren't you the least bit curious what's inside you?

AMANDA: There is no human being in here!

CYNTHIA: Well, what's in there then? Malibu Barbie?

AMANDA: It becomes a human being when it leaves my womb! That's just common sense!

CYNTHIA: What if it's a preemie and has to be delivered fourteen weeks before its due date?

AMANDA: Then that's when it's a human being—

CYNTHIA: So what's the deciding factor—air?

AMANDA: Huh? *(To audience)* Huh?

CYNTHIA: When the fetus hits air, boom, it's suddenly a human being? Whether it's nine months or three weeks after conception? What kind of Fourth Century science is that? What do you call the thing inside you that's been eating, shitting, and kicking its legs till it hits the magical air?

AMANDA: *(To* CYNTHIA*)* It can't live on its own—

CYNTHIA: Neither can a two-year old. Should we be allowed to kill two-year olds, too?

AMANDA: What are you, the fucking Taliban?

CYNTHIA: That's a living, breathing human being in there, Amanda!

AMANDA: It is not!

CYNTHIA: You're a murderer! A godless murderer!

AMANDA: The fuck I am! You are! And I'm gonna kill you!

(AMANDA *and* CYNTHIA *each grab a kitchen knife as they did at the beginning of the act.*)

CYNTHIA: And I'm gonna kill you!

AMANDA: You can't just yell me out of an abortion!

CYNTHIA: Why won't you give up?

AMANDA: Why won't you give up?

CYNTHIA: Because I'm trying to save your daughter's life! Top that!

AMANDA: Because I'm trying to save my life! Top that! *(A moment. To audience)* And that's where you came in. *(To* CYNTHIA, *tossing down her knife)* Okay. You're booked.

CYNTHIA: What?

AMANDA: Booked. On my show. Radio and T V.

CYNTHIA: Never.

AMANDA: What?

CYNTHIA: That's a sucker's game. Victory always goes to the media savvy, not to the righteous position. You sway the studio audience, the studio audience sways the viewer. I'm better one on one—no cameras or mics.

AMANDA: You mean...this whole act wasn't an audition?

CYNTHIA: No—wasnj't an audition, wasn't an act! Amazing how indifference to fame bewilders show people. I don't want to break your heart, but I'm a little more substantial than that.

AMANDA: But everyone wants to get on my show!

CYNTHIA: 'Cept me and Christopher Hitchens.

AMANDA: Then what are you doing here?

CYNTHIA: Don't you get it? I'm here to make sure Amanda Junior is born. And have dinner.

AMANDA: If that's why you're here, you've really wasted your time. Everything you've said so far has persuaded me I should have two abortions. Now if you'd like to join me in a glass of 2004 Corton-Charlemagne to celebrate your first defeat, please do so, but then you must be on your way.

CYNTHIA: Abortion gives you breast cancer!

AMANDA: Bullshit!

CYNTHIA: Early Alzheimer's!

AMANDA: Bullshit!

CYNTHIA: Skin breaks out in boils!

AMANDA: Double bullshit!

CYNTHIA: Well, it works on some people

AMANDA: But you can say it all you want on my show.

CYNTHIA: Are you kidding? It'd be like going on the Ellen Degeneres Show and saying lesbianism is the devil's work—
(To audience) —which it is by the way.
(To AMANDA) You're N P R, ground zero for partisanship in sheep's clothing, where every damn one of you sounds like you went to Mount Holyoke—

AMANDA: There are men at N P R.

CYNTHIA: It's the men I'm talking about.

AMANDA: So the men on N P R are all gay? Haven't you ever heard *Car Talk*?

CYNTHIA: They may all be hetero horndogs, but they sure sound like they've had too many women professors. One thing I hate, it's sensitive men. Joyless and smug. Men and women. National Pussy Radio is what my son Jordan calls it.

AMANDA: Look, Cynthia, I admire your commitment, but I can't have a baby right now.

CYNTHIA: Why not?

AMANDA: This situation was a result of rape.

CYNTHIA: Rape?

(ROBERT enters in a rage.)

ROBERT: Did she tell you it was rape yet?

CYNTHIA: Whoa, yeah, she—

AMANDA: Robert, what are you doing back?

ROBERT: Kit told me she was a baby doctor, it took me half a martini to figure it out! Rape—that's what she claimed the day after! Know what the rape was? Two consenting adults yearning for each other, having shared a full, rich sexual life for ten years, then separated for two months, getting together for dinner, right at this table—*this table*—and she plies me with— get this—shepherd's pie, my favorite food in the world, and two great bottles of '04 Corton-Charlemagne, her favorite food in the world, and lights get dimmed, Michael Buble's somehow on the stereo, everybody starts panting, eyelids lower, clothes peel off—

(KIT enters unseen by the others, sits and watches.)

AMANDA: You were very forceful—

ROBERT: Forceful? You're a vegan! You served me shepherd's pie! What could be more seductive than a vegan serving ground meat? The submission, the sacrifice...she might as well have given me a lap dance—which she subsequently did, by the way. This wasn't rape, it wasn't even date rape, it wasn't even kiss rape. You wanted to get it on just as much as I did, maybe more—

AMANDA: Just because I wanted to against my better judgment was no reason for you to take advantage of me.

ROBERT: See what she does—twists your mind into a sailing knot! *(Noticing* KIT*)* Hey Wonder Woman, would you mind leaving us alone for a couple of minutes? I'm sorry I had to interrupt our dinner, but this was important. We'll go get you some in a couple of minutes.

KIT: I want to stay.

AMANDA: No you don't. Go to your room.

ROBERT: Yeah, you better, dude.

KIT: If *you* say so, Daddy. *(She exits.)*

ROBERT: Well?

AMANDA: It doesn't matter, Robert. You're not involved.

ROBERT: Not involved? Whose baby do you think this is?

AMANDA: It's not a baby, and whatever it is, it no longer has anything to do with you. Now please, this woman was just on her way out—

ROBERT: This isn't just about you! I'm the father, the donor, you couldn't have this thing without me—

AMANDA: Well I can *not* have it without you. Come on, you don't want a baby—

ROBERT: You don't know that. You know how much I love Kit—

AMANDA: Yes, once a week you love her very much, maybe you will two weeks in the summer, we'll see. And you were wonderful in the hospital. But that was seven years ago.

ROBERT: *(Tearing up)* She was so lovely! Those precious feet...saucer eyes...

AMANDA: You're a great Disneyland GlamDad, Robert, but somehow between the day we left the hospital and this very moment, you haven't been very attentive. And now suddenly you're Father of the Year and all against abortion—

ROBERT: I'm totally in favor of abortion. Sometimes I think there should be more abortions—

CYNTHIA: But you don't want your daughter aborted.

ROBERT: Daughter? You already know it's a girl? Oh my God, fifteen minutes ago I didn't even know it was a thing of any kind, and now it's my daughter! Amanda, we always talked about having another one for Kit to grow up with.

AMANDA: That was a hundred years ago, Robert. Please, you don't want a baby boy or girl, and it's not necessarily a girl—

CYNTHIA: Oh yes it is! And now you're in favor of life.

ROBERT: Of course I'm in favor of life—my daughter's life.

AMANDA: Oh, stop being so ridiculously male! You get an impulse, you think you have to act on it. Want to get laid, don't think about the consequences, all you flash on is "Vulva, vulva!" Idyllic fantasticals about raising a little girl, don't realize it's eighteen to twenty-one years on call all day. All that sanctimonious bullshit about the nobility of parenthood. All crawling and pooping little Freudian *ids* make you carry them when they can perfectly well walk, never get over themselves till they've got kids of their own. What's so glamorous and romantic about wrecking your body and giving yourself over to ungrateful and self-centered little shits who think the world revolves around them? People have kids because they don't want to be alone when their spouses die or because they're so vain they want clones so the next generation won't forget them. *(To* CYNTHIA*)* Even you played to my vanity. "She'll have your speech intonations," and your nose, and your knees, and if you can only shape them right, your politics and religion.

CYNTHIA: My God...you hate kids!

AMANDA: I do not. They're just over-rated. I'm going to take up smoking. I love and will raise and protect Kit. But I won't love, raise, and protect a sex accident, and this is a sex accident.

ROBERT: Did you ever think it might be a divine accident?

AMANDA: Robert, you're an atheist!

ROBERT: Not about everything. You just can't do this alone, Amanda, not without even consulting me—

AMANDA: Okay, Robert, I'll consult you: I'll have this baby. I'll have your little darling. And the moment I'm out of the hospital, I will put her in a little basket and give her to your doorman. I'll sign a piece of paper that says she is yours one hundred percent, that I will never see her, talk to her, text her, have no rights to her whatever, and you can raise her any way you want— walk her to pre-K every day for three years, limo her to Dalton or let her crawl to P S 85, third-degree her every boyfriend or underwrite her heroin addiction and let her B F F with the Kardashians. Spoil her rotten or turn her over to Tough Love Nanny, get her the Nobel in physics or ignore her and ruin her life. She will be one hundred percent yours. Twenty-one years of rapturous fatherhood bliss. I'm consulting you, Robert. Want this little adorable?

ROBERT: Uh...I'm pretty over-extended as it is.

AMANDA: Yes, yes, Robert, you are pretty over-extended. Now how should we proceed, because I'm very very pregnant. What do you suggest since neither you nor I want to bring a child into this world or to take care of one?

ROBERT: Well, maybe an abortion...?

AMANDA: Good idea! You've given me advice I never could have reached on my own. And now our real existing daughter is starving.

ROBERT: There's something wrong with this—you shouldn't just be able to dispose of our daughter on your own.

AMANDA: Oh yes I should. Big "Yes I should."

ROBERT: (*To* CYNTHIA) And you—you're going to do this?

CYNTHIA: Mister Morosini, I don't think you understand—

ROBERT: Abortions may be necessary, admirable even, but that doesn't mean the butchers who perform them are honorable or moral or anything but vermin, and when I think of you destroying my daughter—!

(ROBERT *loses it, shrieks, and attacks* CYNTHIA.)

(KIT *runs in. Much screaming*)

KIT: Daddy! Daddy!

AMANDA: (*Pulling him off* CYNTHIA) She's not an abortionist! She's not an abortionist!

ROBERT: She's not?

AMANDA: No.

ROBERT: My God, I'm so sorry. I didn't know—I assumed—

CYNTHIA: It's all right. The issue really brings out the emotions.

AMANDA: She is personally responsible for at least sixteen out of twenty onsite clinic conversions and has a personal success rating of one hundred percent.

ROBERT: You're trying to talk her out of having an abortion?

CYNTHIA: Yes sir.

ROBERT: You go everywhere with this message?

CYNTHIA: Everywhere I can.

ROBERT: That is the most reprehensible thing I've ever heard! How can you do that? I fucking hate right-wing Christian fascist pro-lifers!

(ROBERT *shrieks and attacks* CYNTHIA *exactly the same way.* AMANDA *and* KIT *pull him off her again.*)

AMANDA: Robert! Robert!

KIT: Daddy! Daddy!

(AMANDA *smashes a dish, retrieves a knife, and threatens* ROBERT.)

AMANDA: Knock it off, Robert!

(ROBERT *releases* CYNTHIA.)

AMANDA: Now that's enough! Robert, I don't love you. You also don't love me.

KIT: I'm hungry.

AMANDA: You're not going out with Daddy tonight, honey. Please go to your room. We'll make sandwiches.

ROBERT: Yeah, we'll catch up next week, doofus.

KIT: You're a doofus!

ROBERT: Oh, I forgot—I've got to go to Dallas. The week after, doofus times ten. Good night, precious child.

KIT: G'night, doofus times infinity. *(She exits.)*

ROBERT: *(To* AMANDA*)* And you, you'll spend the rest of your life in the flaming bowels and boiler rooms of hell on earth!
(To CYNTHIA*)* Right next to her!
(To AMANDA*)* Wait'll the judge hears about this—then we'll see who gets the co-op! *(He exits.)*

CYNTHIA: I sense ambivalence.

AMANDA: I sense assholeosity.

AMANDA: How's your throat?

CYNTHIA: I'm used to worse. He has the soft, mean hands of a lawyer.

AMANDA: Hedge fund manager.

CYNTHIA: So it wasn't exactly rape.

AMANDA: And abortions don't give you breast cancer.

CYNTHIA: You know, in a parallel universe we might have been friends.

AMANDA: Think?

CYNTHIA: Robert isn't a very believable rapist.

AMANDA: Listen, l am in awe of your life, Cynthia. I am. Young, lost woman finds love, God, family, her own self-worth. *Lifetime* and *Oxygen* channels combined. That was your choice, go with God. But you must respect this is mine. I hate abortion! It's not something I want to do. It's the least worst thing I can think of.

CYNTHIA: Nope, we couldn't have been friends in any universe, parallel or otherwise, and I don't have to respect that choice at all.

AMANDA: I'm not raising another child if she turns out to be Anna Deavere fucking Sarandon!

CYNTHIA: But nobody's asking you to raise a child.

AMANDA: Hm?

CYNTHIA: Just give birth to one.

AMANDA: What?

CYNTHIA: *(Coming closer)* There are hundreds of thousands of people in this country alone dying to raise your beautiful child, Amanda. Right now they have to go to Romania to get them.

AMANDA: But that would be agony.

CYNTHIA: No it wouldn't. I've done it dozens of times. I'll make the transition after childbirth so easy you won't miss her, you won't get depressed, you'll be filled with the love of whatever god you believe in, and if there isn't one, the void you adore. You'll feel joy pounding in every vein!

AMANDA: I thought we regressives at N P R don't feel joy.

CYNTHIA: You'll be the first.

AMANDA: But...give up my own baby?

CYNTHIA: What do you think you'll be doing if you choose abortion?

(AMANDA thinks this over for a second.)

AMANDA: What if she's got Down's Syndrome?

CYNTHIA: We've got families who'll raise kids with two heads.

AMANDA: My mother would kill me. I would kill me. I will not be powerless! I will not sanction bloody coat hanger murders!

CYNTHIA: Hey, I know what went on before *Roe v Wade*, only from underneath. I had the *not* Mount Holyoke perspective. I didn't think it was murder then, just bloody, but I sure do think it's murder now!

(AMANDA *ruminates.*)

AMANDA: All right, Cynthia, you know what? You're right. It is alive, and it is murder! Murder murder murder! Buzz word buzz word buzz word! And you know what? I don't give a shit.

CYNTHIA: Whoa...you mean you're saying...it's murder and that's okay?

AMANDA: Yup. Now what?

CYNTHIA: Hunh. So...

AMANDA: So it's unimportant murder. That is my final conclusion. It's not meaningful murder any more than shooting ptarmigan is.

CYNTHIA: Will you go on the air and say that?

AMANDA: No.

CYNTHIA: Because I'll be your guest if you will.

AMANDA: No way on heaven and earth. It would be colossally misunderstood. Now you have heard my conclusion. End of conversation, end of visit. Good-bye, "Doctor" Rense, ha-ha. Now Kit likes it when we make meat-laden roast beef sandwiches together. (*She exits with sandwich ingredients on a tray.*)

CYNTHIA: Murder is okay? I do calisthenics with "It's not alive." I can easily handle "I don't want this, can't afford this, used to love his daddy but no longer do, hey, I'm underage, I was forced, it was Ruffies", or even, "I've got a radio show and I'm too busy." I can

deal with all that. All the domestic imperialism—
rationalizing executions of a billion babies since time
began. But...it's murder, and it's okay? Staggering.
Brilliant, sort of. Except...except...I don't think so... *(She
looks around)* Adapt. Adapt. Steady, steady.

*(CYNTHIA grinds pills in the food processor, pours the
resulting powder into the wok; adds a big scoop of habaneros
to cover the taste. She dims lights; tosses an onion into the
processor just as AMANDA enters.)*

AMANDA: What are you doing?

CYNTHIA: Just helping out. Everybody always needs an
onion. Sit down. You've had a hard day.

(CYNTHIA helps AMANDA into a chair.)

AMANDA: Listen, would you mind terribly if we
didn't—

CYNTHIA: I'd so like it if we could share a meal. We
won't talk about pro-life and pro-choice or children or
the afterlife. I respect your decision.

AMANDA: You do? You mean...I really am your first
defeat?

CYNTHIA: My first defeat.

AMANDA: Wow. Why can't I get this on tape? But I'm
so exhausted, I couldn't reheat coffee in the microwave.

CYNTHIA: I'll make it, if you don't mind an enthusiastic
amateur invading the kitchen of a pro. *(She ladles the
mallum into a mug, hands it to AMANDA.)*

AMANDA: The way I feel, a bowl of Captain Crunch
will be just fine.

CYNTHIA: The mallum will relax you. Tell you what,
You go ahead and eat, I'll cook my birds in it in a few
minutes.

AMANDA: Then how will you tell your grandkids I cooked dinner for you?

CYNTHIA: I'll lie to the little motherfuckers. They'll probably be a pain in the ass anyway.

AMANDA: *(Sipping mallum)* Wow—you like habaneros even more than I do. But it's very tasty.

CYNTHIA: I always serve soup in a mug. Gives me such a glow right in my colon when I chug it.

(AMANDA chugs it. CYNTHIA ladles another, hands it to AMANDA. She drinks it.)

AMANDA: Yeah...I can't believe it—your first defeat. How do you feel?

CYNTHIA: I'm a big girl. Would you like some more coconut? I love coconut.

AMANDA: Sure, so do I.

(CYNTHIA adds coconut to the third mug, replaces it when AMANDA finishes the second.)

AMANDA: *(Starting to feel the drug)* Hey, what if Jeeeezus was adopted?

CYNTHIA: Jesus—whipping boy of western comedy. Jesus can be adopted, Jesus can be psycho, Jesus can be homo. Jesus can have secret kids. "We found Jesus's bones—he couldn't've ascended into heaven!" Big yucks. But say one word about Mohammed marrying that six year-old—World War Nine.

(CYNTHIA hands AMANDA a new mug.)

AMANDA: You shoo be happy about that Cynthie baby. It's shows how crazy they are and why we're cooler. Hey, you're not cooking your ptarmi—...ptarmi—

CYNTHIA: Ptarmigan. You don't have to look if you don't want to.

AMANDA: I can take a li'l ole ptarmi— ...ptarmi—
...why can't I say this? Bird! This hip is really very
really...hurts hard... *(She pops a pill; drinks from wine
bottle.)*

CYNTHIA: Here, I'll do that, you sit down and relax
after what I put you through.

*(CYNTHIA helps AMANDA sit, then fills a pot with water,
puts knives in it, places it over high heat.)*

AMANDA: *(Delirious)* What we both put each other
through. You know, for a Pol Pot right wing fascisto,
you...can be...take...must be...very good care of those
kidlets. Babylets. Blankets. All those beautiful babylet
blanketines. And trumpets. All those trumpets! Brass
of all kinds. Danny Boy Pistol Pump. Very considerate,
you. See, cook on radio, people have to visualize, use
their noggin, imagination, grab their imagination! The
trick. You got 'em. Ho hooeyhey! You got 'em! Got me?
(Blindly) Ho, hey, you...boiling knives?

CYNTHIA: Can't be too careful.

AMANDA: Where's my kidney? Whadduz this sex
stallion Danny-o Ho Dabby Boy, the pipes, the pipes
are caaa-lling, the pipes...Dabby smoke a pipe? Or
Dabby a plubber? Gives you so many kids—hey, you
know all your kids' names come from the Bible?

CYNTHIA: Yes.

AMANDA: Jordash, Gobitha, Noah's Ark, Magdalene
known as Maggie, Pintarina, Zeus, Amphitryon,
Gorbo, DOUG, Ruth, oh, Ruuuuth—

CYNTHIA: Yes.

AMANDA: Ho hey, hip for my pill. Gimme a hip for
my pill! He Dabby give you all your trillionomics or
is there much more out there than ever I wouldda
suspected in fighting abortions? I wanna get a hip
for my pill. Ruuuuuub it riiiiiight into the socket....

Whuzzz...whuzz goin' on? Wha' ya doin'—boilin' mah knives...?

CYNTHIA: One had a really bad stain.

(AMANDA stands, then suddenly collapses completely, knocking over a glass and a chair. She is one-eighth conscious.)

CYNTHIA: Here let me help you.

(CYNTHIA fetches a cushion for AMANDA.)

AMANDA: Yes, I...whuzz...happenin', bro'?

CYNTHIA: Good girl, you're such a good girl...

(CYNTHIA washes her hands with Corton Charlemagne. She grabs a knife, briefly prays, then falls to her knees with the knife and performs a C-Section on AMANDA. This can be done in plain view or in dim light or behind furniture. As CYNTHIA brings another life into the world, AMANDA wakes—)

AMANDA: Owww! Hey, hey—!

CYNTHIA: 's okay, 's okay, Mandy, you won't feel a thing—

(CYNTHIA tugs and tugs. After a few moments, a baby cries. She wraps it and may reveal it to the audience. She is sweating and her hands are bloodied. She's exhausted but filled with joy. Suddenly she sees something else in AMANDA.)

CYNTHIA: Oh my God. You dear, dear God...

(CYNTHIA falls to her knees, tugs again...and a second baby cries.)

(KIT enters with a half-eaten sandwich.)

KIT: Hey, why's Mommy like that?

(CYNTHIA gets between KIT and AMANDA.)

CYNTHIA: Don't come any closer, Kit. Your mommy's in trouble, but she'll be fine if you just do exactly as I tell you.

KIT: What is it, what is it!

CYNTHIA: Be very calm, Kit or you won't be helping Mommy. Do as I tell you—I'm a doctor—and Mommy will be all right. Now pick up the phone and dial 9-1-1.

KIT: But why's—

CYNTHIA: Please dial 9-1-1. Speak very clearly and calmly.

(KIT *punches 9-1-1 into the phone.*)

KIT: *(Into phone)* Kit Morosini. Seven.

(CYNTHIA *is clear and distinct and is busy keeping the newborns warm.*)

CYNTHIA: Tell them a doctor is telling you what to do, this is a matter of life and death.

KIT: A doctor is here telling me what to do. This is a matter of life and death.

CYNTHIA: Please send an ambulance to 145 Central Park West—

KIT: Please send an ambulance to 145 Central Park West—

CYNTHIA: —equipped with two preemie resuscitators

KIT: —weenie?

CYNTHIA: —preemie—

KIT: —preemie—

CYNTHIA: —re-

KIT: —re—

CYNTHIA: —susc—

KIT: —susc—

CYNTHIA: —itators.

KIT: —itators. —Re-susc-itators—

CYNTHIA: Incubators, warmers, infant I Vs—

KIT: Incubators, warmers, infant I Ds—

CYNTHIA: —not I Ds, I Vs—

KIT: —I Vs, not I Ds, sorry—

CYNTHIA: That's okay, dear. Also, equipment to bring the pressure up.

KIT: Equipment to bring the pressure up.

CYNTHIA: Excellent. It's a matter of life and death.

KIT: It's an urgent matter of life and death.

CYNTHIA: Good, urgent, good. Hang up.

KIT: *(Hangs up)* What is it?

CYNTHIA: You're a wonderful girl, Kit, and you did a wonderful job. It was very important you spoke so precisely and articulately. Be very kind to your mother Kit, because she's been through hell. But I've patched her up, and she'll be fine. Because she was willing to go through the fight of her life—

(CYNTHIA *raises the twins above her head in beatific light.)*

CYNTHIA: —you now have an adorable little sister and an adorable little brother.

KIT: No way!

CYNTHIA: Yes. And mother and babies are doing fine.

(Blackout)

Epilogue

(In the dark)

(Sounds of ambulance, walkie-talkie rasps, E R Commands, then the soothing music of Michael Buble and a heart monitor.)

(Lights up on)

(AMANDA lying asleep in a hospital bed, a twin under each arm. She is surrounded by KIT, ROBERT, and CYNTHIA, all smiling and in hospital gowns and caps, maybe masks around their necks. AMANDA awakes, sees her surroundings, then each of her nemeses, wonders why they're smiling. The babies cry. The bed tilts so AMANDA is almost upright. She looks at the babies, realizes what her life will be, and screams—.)

AMANDA: YAAAAAHHHHHHH!

(Blackout)

(Fast curtain)

END OF PLAY